THE WORDS OF
AFRICAN-AMERICAN
HEROES

THE WORDS OF
AFRICAN-AMERICAN HEROES

Selected and with an
Introduction by
Clara Villarosa

Newmarket Press
New York

The Newmarket "Words Of" Series

This book is published in the United States of America and Canada.

ISBN 978-1-55704-945-2 (paperback) 10 9 8 7 6 5 4 3 2 1
ISBN 978-1-55704-946-9 (hardcover) 10 9 8 7 6 5 4 3 2 1

Library of Congress Cataloging-in-Publication Data

The words of African-American heroes / selected and with an introduction by Clara Villarosa.
     p. cm.
  Includes index.
  ISBN 978-1-55704-945-2 (alk. paper)
  1. African Americans--Quotations. I. Villarosa, Clara.
  PN6081.3.W66 2011
  081.089'96073--dc22

                                        2010050084

QUANTITY PURCHASES
Companies, professional groups, clubs, and other organizations may qualify for special terms when ordering quantities of this title. For information, e-mail sales@newmarketpress.com; or write to Special Sales Department, Newmarket Press, 18 East 48th Street, New York, NY 10017; call (212) 832-3575 ext. 19 or 1-800-669-3903; fax (212) 832-3629.

Manufactured in the United States of America

www.newmarketpress.com

CONTENTS

INTRODUCTION

BY CLARA VILLAROSA

When I was asked by Newmarket Press to select quotations for a book entitled *The Words of African-American Heroes,* I must admit I was both surprised and flattered. However, I was hesitant. I was a retired bookseller. Within the last year I had written and published a book called *Down to Business: The First 10 Steps of Entrepreneurship for Women*, with my daughter Alicia. I was enjoying my retirement after sixteen years in the book business. I had not considered embarking on another book project. But after giving it some thought, I decided to take on the project. I had to collect and edit the words of other people. Now, how difficult could that be?

Having accepted the challenge, I learned a great deal in the process of doing my research and further improved my editing skills. The first step was coming up with criteria for identifying and selecting the African-American heroes and sheroes. The dictionary defines a "hero" as a person distinguished by exceptional courage, ability, and fortitude; one who is idolized, admired, and, in the opinion of others, highly regarded; one who is a role model and possesses superior qualities. While not every one of my selections may embody each of these qualities, all are certainly considered heroes by the people who know them. As the founder of the Hue-Man Book Store, which specializes in books by and about African Americans, I had hosted many author events, and therefore I am familiar with or have personally met a large number of distinguished African Americans.

In developing a list of heroes, I wanted to make sure that

women were well represented and also to include heroes from a variety of occupations and fields of interest. As I proceeded with this collection of quotations, I realized how much additional information and history I was learning about my subjects. I became more informed about their work, talent, and circumstances. The words were actually inspiring me to work on the project. I found myself becoming more informed and inspired, and I hope this is the very purpose of this book for its readers.

I discovered a range of the words representing a broad spectrum of heroes from many different situations and circumstances whose accomplishments are truly remarkable. I came to understand that the selections had to resonate with readers, withstand the test of time, and hopefully stick and be remembered. I came up with some surprising quotes from expected and unexpected heroes. Some examples include Carole Gist, the first African American to capture the title of Miss USA, who was pleased about laying the groundwork for others; Romare Bearden, who explained the process of creation in the context of being influenced by other artists; Matthew Henson, who was grateful for representing his race standing on the North Pole; Harriet Tubman, who expressed regret for not being able to take more slaves to freedom because of their attitudes; and Condoleezza Rice and Colin Powell, the first two African Americans to serve as Secretary of State, who each gave very much the same advice on the handling of life's crises.

The themes for the chapters were based on the predominant preoccupations of the quotes from my initial list of heroes. Their words fell into certain categories, and as I came across new memorable quotes, the process became easier to identify which theme they exemplified. I also wanted the chapters to have titles that represented contemporary language that young people could relate to, while clearly describing the themes of the book.

I was inspired by some previous collections, including *Quotations in Black* and *Contemporary Quotations in Black,* both edited by Anita King; *Words to Make My Dream Children Live: A Book of African American Quotations,* edited by Deirdre Mullane; and *My Soul Looks Back, 'Less I Forget: A Collection of Quotations by People of Color*, edited by Dorothy Winbush Riley. I appreciate these editors' tireless work and extensive compilation of materials. I myself spent hours in the Schomburg Center for Research in Black Culture, completing my own research in that fine collection of original source material.

With the biographical notes in the back of the book, the reader has the opportunity to obtain additional information about each hero and to place the sayings in context. One can be reflective about not just *what* you know but *how* you know the person. The quotations span the breadth of the history of African Americans, from slavery, emancipation, Reconstruction, Jim Crow, the Harlem Renaissance, civil rights, right up to the hip-hop generation. The bios needed to be brief but contain information for the reader to understand why the heroes were selected. Many of those listed were the first African Americans in their particular field of accomplishment. It was surprising to see how many were educated at Ivy League schools, and yet many others were not given the opportunity to have even a basic education. Some come from humble backgrounds and had to overcome tremendous odds. Others were motivated by negative experiences and wanted to rectify these wrongs in society.

Education proves a key component in the lives of all of these heroes, and we must ensure the good education of our youth to give us more heroes. Young readers can set higher standards for themselves when they are inspired by the achievements of those listed here. Reading about heroes not only added to my knowledge but inspired me to reach for higher goals. If they did it, so can I, and so can you.

I hope that readers will not only learn from these memorable quotations but will be stimulated to share them with friends and family, and, of course, to pick up related books to get more information about our heroes and black history. Who knows, maybe there will be heroes reading this book whose words will be recorded in future printings.

1.

SPARKING THE
IMAGINATION:
CREATIVITY
AND ART

ROMARE BEARDEN

"Practically all the great artists have accepted the influence of others. But the difference lies in the fact that the artist with vision sees his material, chooses, changes, and, by integrating what he has learned with his own experiences, finally molds something distinctly personal."

"The Negro Artist and Modern Art,"
Opportunity, December 1934

"I create social identities so far as the subjects are Negro, but I have not created protest images, because the world within the collage, if it is authentic, retains the right to speak for itself."

Art News, October 1964

ELIZABETH CATLETT

"Sometimes I put things away because I become frustrated to the point where I should not make decisions. This type of antagonism can be the root of creativity because it leads you to closer examinations of your approach and to alternative solutions to problems."

The Art of Elizabeth Catlett, 1984

JAMES WELDON JOHNSON

"A people may become great through many means, but there is only one measure by which its greatness is recognized and acknowledged. The final measure of greatness of all peoples is the amount and standard of the literature and art they have produced."

The Book of African American Negro Poetry, 1922

"In a word, the stereotype is that the Negro is nothing more than a beggar at the gate of the nation, waiting to be thrown crumbs of civilization. Through his artistic efforts the Negro is smashing this immemorial stereotype faster than he has ever done through any other method he has been able to use. He is making it realized that he is the possessor of a wealth of natural endowments and that he has long been a generous giver to America. He is impressing upon the national mind the conviction that he is an active and important force in American life; that he is a creator as well as a creature; that he has given as well as received; that he is the potential giver of larger and richer contributions."

Harper's Magazine, 1925

ANGELA DAVIS

"Progressive art can assist people to learn not only about the objective forces at work in the society in which they live, but also about the intensely social character of their interior lives. Ultimately, it can propel people toward social emancipation."

Art on the Frontline, 1984

HENRY LOUIS GATES

"In literacy lay freedom for the black slave. . . . No group of slaves anywhere at any other period in history has left such a large repository of testimony about the horror of becoming the legal property of another human being. This was no easy task. Nevertheless, the ex-slave met this challenge squarely, creating the largest body of literature ever created by ex-slaves and giving birth thereby to the Afro-American literary tradition."

The Classic Slave Narratives, 1987

PAULE MARSHALL

"They had taken a language imposed upon them, and infused it with their own incisive rhythms and syntax, brought to bear upon it the few African words and sounds that had been retained and made it their own."

New Letter, 1973

MALCOLM GLADWELL

"Good writing does not succeed or fail on the strength of its ability to persuade. It succeeds or fails on the strength of its ability to engage you, to make you think, to give you a glimpse into someone else's head."

What the Dog Saw and Other Adventures, 2009

TERRY MCMILLAN

"If you're lucky enough to be given a voice that people want to listen to, I think you ought to use it to say something important."

Ebony, May 1993

OCTAVIA BUTLER

"A science-fiction writer has the freedom to do absolutely anything. The limits are in the imagination of the writer."

Black Scholar, March–April 1986

ISHMAEL REED

"Regardless of the criticisms I receive from the left, the right, and the middle, I think it's important to maintain a prolific writing jab, as long as my literary legs hold up."

Writin' Is Fightin', 1988

"Writing has made me a better man. It has put me in contact with those fleeing moments which prove the existence of soul."
African American Writers, 1991

"Afro-American literature is food for a deep lifetime study, not something to be squeezed into a quarter or a semester."

"It may turn out that the great restive underground language rising from the American slums and fringe communities is the real American poetry and prose, that can tell you the way things are happening now."
New Black Voices, 1972

NIKKI GIOVANNI
"That's why literature is so important. We cannot possibly leave it to history as a discipline, not to sociology nor science nor economics to tell the story of our people. . . . It's not a ladder we're climbing, it's literature we are producing and there will always be someone to read it."
Black Women Writers, 1984

RITA DOVE
"Poetry is language at its most distilled and most powerful . . . you carry it around and then it nourishes you when you need it."
Washington Post, May 19, 1993

ALICE WALKER
"Poetry, I have discovered, is always unexpected and always as faithful and honest as dreams."
We Have a Beautiful Mother, 1981

NTOZAKE SHANGE

"I'm a playwright. But I'm a woman first . . . a woman playwright. And I would hope that my choice of words and my choice of characters and situations reflect my experience as a woman on the planet. I don't have anything that I can add to the masculine perception of the world. What I can add has to be from what I've experienced. And my perceptions and my syntax, my colloquialisms, my preoccupations, are founded on race and gender."

The New York Times, May 7, 1989

SONIA SANCHEZ

"I write to tell the truth about the Black condition as I see it. Therefore I write to offer a Black woman's view of the world. . . . So the values in my work reflect the values I live by and work for. I keep writing because I realize that until Black people's social reality is free of oppression and exploitation, I will not be free to write as one who's not oppressed or exploited. That is the goal. That is the struggle and the dream."

Black Women Writers, 1984

PEARL CLEAGE

"The theatre is for me—a hollering place. A place to talk about our black female lives, defined by our specific black female reality to each other first and then to others of good will who will take the time to listen and understand."

Speech given at Literary Managers and Dramaturgs of the America, *LMDA Review,* June 1994

"As a playwright I don't want to spend all my time fussing at white racism, but as a feminist, I don't want to spend all my time fussing at men. . . . The responsibility is to tell the complete truth, and if you do that, the whole question of role models is really moot."

American Theatre, July/August 1996

ELLA FITZGERALD

"I guess what everyone wants more than anything else is to be loved. And to know you have loved me for my singing is too much for me. Forgive me if I don't have the words. Maybe I can sing and you'll understand."

In an awards ceremony celebrating her first two decades of show business, *Newsweek,* June 7, 1954

DEBBIE ALLEN

"I pounded pavements and went to every audition. That was my spirit. Work at whatever you do, whether you get paid or not."

Parade, November 17, 1991

ODETTA

"Through singing I continue to find myself, and the more I find myself, the less I have to deny other people themselves."

I Dream a World, 1989

TINA TURNER
"Sometimes you've got to let everything go . . . purge your-self. I did that. . . . If you are unhappy with anything . . . bringing you down, get rid of it. Because you'll find that when you're free, your true creativity, your true self comes out. So there I was dealing with me. . . . I had talent . . . and I never allowed myself to get lost. I held on to the positive. I gave into myself. I went inside of me to help me. It can hap-pen."

"As long as I am alive, why not keep living as beautifully as you can. It's not a matter of money. Success has brought me many material things . . . success has been useful to me and to the people I love. . . . My career is still in bloom and I'm ripe enough to teach anybody. I'll tell what I've learned. Many of you will listen, and some of you will hear."

I, Tina, 1986

GREGORY HINES
"The best entertainment speaks to the human condition in an honest way."

Parade, May 31, 1992

MICHAEL JACKSON
"The same music governs the rhythm of seasons, the pulse of our heartbeats, the migration of birds, the ebb and flow of ocean tides, the cycles of growth, evolution and dissolution. It's music, it's rhythm."

Michael Jackson: In His Own Words, 1993

"My goal in life is to give the world what I have been lucky to receive: the ecstasy of divine union through my music and dance."

Interview with Oprah Winfrey, February 1993

JANET JACKSON
"I don't believe in luck. It's hard work and not forgetting your dream—and going after it. It's about still having hunger in your heart."

Ebony, September 1993

VIRGINIA JOHNSON
"I had an interview with the paper in Sacramento. It was a little frustrating trying to explain how much we were all setting out to be ballet dancers, not just black ballet dancers. As if being born black meant being in a cage and your entire life would be described by that cage. The interviewer, being white and never having experienced that kind of limitation, could not understand."

Personal journal entry, January 20, 1988,
printed in *The New York Times,* March 6, 1994

EDDIE MURPHY
"It's not the public that inspired an artist to create. An artist feels the need to create even if there is no public. If there were no one on the planet I'd still do funny things. I'd just be laughing by myself."

Playboy, February 1990

"An artist has to stay true to himself as an artist. That is the only obligation he has—to his art. And if you are focused on that, it will touch people."

Newsday, June 28, 1992

Naomi Sims

"Black women are the most exacting women in the world. We're hard on ourselves. Find quiet time, whether it's for prayer, meditation, cooling out or just thinking cool inner thoughts."

Essence, January 1988

Josephine Baker

"A violinist has his violin, a painter his palette. All I had was myself. I was the instrument that I must care for."

Jazz Cleopatra, 1989

"The rear end exists. I see no reason to be ashamed of it. It's true there are rear ends so stupid, so pretentious, so insignificant that they're good only for sitting on."

Les Memories de Josephine Baker, 1927

"Beautiful? It's all a question of luck. I was born with good legs. As for the rest . . . beautiful, no. Amusing, yes."

Official Josephine Baker Website, circa 1969

GEORGE C. WOLFE
"God created black people and black people created style."
The Gospel according to Miss Roj, from the play
The Colored Museum, 1986

PEARL BAILEY
"My kitchen is a mystical place, a kind of temple for me. It is a place where the surfaces seem to have significance, where the sounds and odors carry meaning that transfers from the past and bridges to the future."

"The fact is that it takes more than ingredients and technique to cook a good meal. A good cook puts something of himself into the preparations—he cooks with enjoyment, anticipation, spontaneity, and he is willing to experiment."
Pearl's Kitchen, 1973

ARETHA FRANKLIN
"I have to really feel a song before I'll deal with it and just about every song I do is based either on an experience I've had or an experience someone I knew had gone through."
Right On, February 1983

"They call me the Lady Soul. . . . Soul is something creative, something active. Soul is honesty, I sing to people about what matters. I sing to the realists, people who accept it like it is. I express problems, there are tears when it's sad and smiles when it's happy. It seems simple to me, but to some, feelings take courage."
Speaking at the Grammy Legends Show, 1991

OSSIE DAVIS
"Being colored can be a lotta fun when ain't nobody lookin'."

"Some of the best pretending in the world is done in front of white folks."

"College ain't so much where you been as how you talk when you get back."

Purlie Victorious, 1961

MAX ROACH
"Jazz is a very democratic musical form. It comes out of communal experience. We take our respective instruments and collectively create a thing of beauty."

Ebony Men, April 1987

QUINCY JONES
"Black music has always been the prologue to social change."

Playboy, July 1990

JOHN COLTRANE
"There is never any end. . . . There are always new sounds to imagine: new feelings to get at. And always, there is the need to keep purifying these feelings and sounds so that we can really see what we've discovered in its pure state. So that we can see more clearly where we are. In that way we can give to those who listen the essence, the best of what we are. But to do that at each stage, we have to keep on cleaning the mirror."

Meditations, 1975

CHARLIE PARKER
"Music is your own experience, your thoughts, your wisdom. If you don't live it, it won't come out of your horn. They teach you there's a boundary line to music. But, man, there's no boundary line to art."

Hear Me Talkin' to Ya 1955

"I realized by using the high notes of the chords as a melodic line, and by the right harmonic progression, I could play what I heard inside me. That's when I was born."

Masters of Jazz, 1991

MILES DAVIS
"There are only two things important to me, and that is music and black people."

Atlantic Constitution, May 27, 1989

"For me, music and life are all about style."

"It's always been a gift with me hearing music the way I do. I don't know where it comes from, it's just there and I don't question it."

"That was my gift . . . having the ability to put certain guys together that would create a chemistry and then letting them go; letting them play what they knew, and above it."

"When you work with great musicians, they are always a part of you . . . their spirits are walking around in me, so they're still here and passing it on to others."

"As a musician and an artist, I have always wanted to reach as many people as I could through my music. And I have never been ashamed of that. Because I never thought that the music called 'jazz' was ever meant to reach just a small group of people, or become a museum thing locked under glass like other dead things that were once considered artistic."

"Bebop was about change, about evolution. It wasn't about standing still and becoming safe. If anybody wants to keep creating they have to be about change."

Miles, 1989

DUKE ELLINGTON

"I live a life of primitivity with the mind of a child and an unquenchable thirst for sharps and flats. The more consonant, the appetizing and delectable they are. . . . Living in a cave, I am almost a hermit, but there is a difference, for I have a mistress. Lovers have come and gone, but my mistress stays. She is beautiful and gentle. She waits on me hand and foot. She is a swinger. She has grace. To hear her speak, you can't believe your ears. She is ten thousand years old. She is as modern as tomorrow, a brand-new woman every day, and as endless as time mathematics. . . . I look forward to her every gesture. Music is my mistress, and she plays second fiddle to no one."

Music Is My Mistress, 1973

LOUIS ARMSTRONG

"Before my time the name was levee camp music, then in New Orleans we called it ragtime. The fantastic music you . . . used to hear 'way back in the old sanctified churches where the sisters would shout till their petticoats fell down."

"I've had some ovations in my time, had beautiful moments, but it seems like I was more content ... growing up in New Orleans, just being around old timers. ... We were poor and everything like that, but music was all around. Music kept you rollin'."

"The main thing is to live for the audience. What you're there for is to please people the best you can. Those few moments belong to them."

LIFE, April 15, 1956

2.

THE TIES
that BIND:
BRANCHES AND LEAVES
OF THE FAMILY TREE

FREDERICK DOUGLASS
"Woman knows and feels her wrongs as man cannot know and feel them, and she also knows as well as he can know, what measures are needed to redress them."
"The Woman's Suffrage Movement Address," published in the *Woman's Journal,* April 14, 1888

CHARLAYNE HUNTER-GAULT
"Whatever I have faced as a woman is probably a lot more subtle than what I have faced as a black person."
I Dream a World, 1989

NIKKI GIOVANNI
"She knows who she is because she knows who she isn't."
Black Women Writers, 1984

PAULA GIDDINGS
"Black women could understand the relationship between racism and sexism because they had to strive against both. In doing so they became the linchpin between two of the most important social reform movements in American history, the struggles for Black rights and women's rights. In the course of defying the imposed limitations on race and sex, they loosened the chains around both."
When and Where I Enter, 1985

DOROTHY HEIGHT
"We African American women seldom do just what we want to do, but always what we have to do."
Inscribed on the Congressional Medal of Honor, presented by President George W. Bush, December 2004

SISTER SOULJAH

"As women, we have the responsibility to correct the things that we do that add to our own oppression."

Playboy, October 1992

SOJOURNER TRUTH

"If the first woman God ever made was strong enough to turn the world upside down all alone, these women together ought to be able to turn it back and get it right side up again."

Address to the fourth National Woman's
Rights Convention, September 7, 1853

"I feel that if I have to answer for the deeds done to my body just as much as a man, I have a right to have just as much as a man. There is a great stir about colored men getting their rights, but not a word about the colored women; and if colored men get their rights, and not colored women theirs, you see the colored men will be masters over the women, and it will be just as bad as it was before."

"I am glad to see that men are getting their rights, but I want women to get theirs, and while the water is stirring I will step into the pool."

"It doesn't seem hard work to vote, though I have seen some men that had a hard time of it."

Address to the First Avenue Meeting of the
American Rights Association, May 3, 1867

JOHNNETTA B. COLE

"The problem with a woman standing behind her man is she can't see where she is going."

Dreams: And Other Lessons of Life, 2001

EARTHA KITT

"It make me furious when I look at women who are in their 50's and 60's and see how beautiful they are at that age, but their beauty isn't readily accepted. Not only do we have savvy, we have knowledge that we did not have before. And we know how to use it."

Ebony, October 1993

JOYCELYN ELDERS

"Black women have always found that in the social order of things we're the least likely to be believed—by anyone."

"You've got to get people's attention before you can achieve change."

The New York Times, January 30, 1994

FAYE WATTLETON

"I do not make any apologies for my manner or my personality. I come from a long line of very strong black Afro-American women who neither bend nor bow. I haven't had very good role models in submission."

"We must trust the people. We must trust each other. We must recognize that private morality should be taught in the home and preached from the pulpit, but it must never be legislated by politicians."

Los Angeles Times, June 19, 1991

HALLE BERRY

"My mother cleared it up for me when I was young. She said when you look in the mirror you're going to see a black woman. You're going to be discriminated against as a black woman so ultimately in this society, that's who you will be. . . . I'm neither black nor white but in the middle. But I needed to make a choice and feel part of this culture. I feel a lot of pride in being a black woman."

Ebony, April 1993

MARY FRANCES BERRY
"The mother-care tradition persists because we are accultur-ated to accept it and because it reinforces existing power arrangements. The tradition is, however, neither tradition nor necessary. . . . There was a time in our country's history when fathers took responsibility for the care of their off-spring. A complete reversal of roles today is neither required nor necessary. If women, however, are to have an equal op-portunity for successful careers and families, both fathers and mothers must share child care."

The Politics of Parenthood, 1993

SADIE AND BESSIE DELANY
"Oh, Mama was a smart woman. It takes a smart woman to fall in love with a good man."

Having Our Say: The Delany Sisters' First 100 Years, 1993

NTOZAKE SHANGE
"Mamas only do things 'cause they love you so much. They can't help it. It's flesh to flesh, blood to blood. No matter how old you get, how grown and on your own, your mama loves you like a newborn."

Betsy Brown, 1985

IDA B. WELLS-BARNETT

"I had already found that motherhood was a profession by itself, just like school teaching and lecturing, and that once one was launched on such a career, she owed it to herself to become as expert as possible in the practice of her profession."

Crusade for Justice, 1991

JESSIE REDMON FAUSET

"All the possibilities of all black men are needed to weld together the black men of the world against the day when black and white meet to do battle. God grant that when that day comes we shall be so powerful that the enemy will say, But behold! These men are our brothers."

The Crisis, November–December 1921

ICE-T

"Because of his upbringing, the ghetto black man has this built-in mechanism he's trying to control. You shouldn't push him toward the edge. Sometimes you're dealing with people who are so frustrated, they are on the brink of insanity."

Playboy, February 1994

BRYANT GUMBEL

"There are very few perceptions in this country that are not tinged by race."

"I think for a number of people, the idea of a secure, confident man who is black is disturbing, and possibly unnerving."

Mirabella, February 1993

SPIKE LEE
"Any black man who is intelligent, opinionated, and who doesn't smile . . . is immediately branded difficult. I'm not difficult, I just know exactly what I want."

Do the Right Thing, 1988

JAMES BROWN
"A man who doesn't stand for something will go for anything."

Los Angeles Times, February 27, 1991

SOLOMON NORTHRUP
"Men may write fictions portraying lowly life as it is, or it is not, may expatiate with owlish gravity upon the bliss of ignorance, discourse flippantly from armchairs of the pleasures of slave life; but let them toil with him in the field, sleep with him in the cabin, feed with him on the husks; let them behold him scourged, hunted, trampled on, and they will come back with another story in their mouths."

Twelve Years a Slave, 1853

H. RAP BROWN
"Being a man is a continuing battle for one's life. One loses a bit of manhood with every stale compromise to the authority of any power in which one does not believe."

Die Nigger Die, 1969

SHIRLEY CHISHOLM

"We have to help black men, but not at the expense of our own personalities as women."

"Women don't get hung up making deals the way men do."
The New York Times, April 13, 1969

"As there are no black Founding Fathers, there were no black founding mothers—a great pity on both counts."
91st Congress *Congressional Record,* August 10, 1979

MARY MCLEOD BETHUNE

"Whatever the achievements of the Negro man in letters, business, art, pulpit, civic progress, and moral reform, he cannot but share them with his sister of darker hue. Whatever glory belongs to the race for a development unprecedented in history . . . a fair share belongs to the womanhood of the race."
Address at the Chicago Women's Federation, June 30, 1935

MALCOLM GLADWELL

"My earliest memories of my father are seeing him work at his desk and realizing that he was happy. I did not know it then, but that was one of the most precious gifts a father can give his child."
Outliers: The Story of Success, 2008

BEBE MOORE CAMPBELL

"Long ago I realized that love is all that is required of fatherhood, that love will spark the action that it takes to mold a child. I have grown strong and whole from the blessings of my many fathers. Everything they gave me—roughness, gruffness, awkward gentleness, the contrast to my female world, their love—is as much a part of me as my bones, my blood. I was given a rich and privileged childhood, an American childhood, a solid foundation on which to stand and, yes, even go forward. I was guided by good men, powerful men. I was raised right. "

Sweet Summer: Growing Up with and without My Dad, 1989

AMIRI BARAKA

"Amina and I are still married and chances are we will be for the rest of our lives. Why? Because we love each other. Despite the sharpness of continuity of our struggles, nothing but love could have held us together under the force of such opposition, though I do not, nor does she, I think, claim invincibility, either in our public or personal lives. But we do claim the emotional, psychological, and intellectual strength to withstand our enemies' designs and learn to live with our own contradictions as a visible confirmation that with all them disagreements, it must be love, like the song says."

The Autobiography of LeRoi Jones, 1997

NINA SIMONE

"The philosophy in our family was that you didn't outshine anyone; you developed the talent you had, but it was there to be shared with everyone else, not hoarded away."

I Put a Spell on You, 1991

SNOOP DOGG

"Parents are teachers. These are people who have knowledge and wisdom and they're trying to pass it on to you. When they give you that, even if you don't like it or understand it—take it for what it's worth because one day you'll hear that voice again and you'll be able to make a decision. You can say, 'I'm going to do the right thing or the wrong thing, but at least I know what the right thing is and the wrong thing is.'"

OK! Magazine, June 15, 2008

RUBY DEE

"The taillights from the kids' cars have disappeared long ago, but our thoughts trailing them have no end. We want them to know that black is a dynamic identity. Black people in America have helped give life to the Constitution. We have helped make it a pulsing, living document. We put justice on the map. We've kept the whole question of human rights alive for this country. We want them to glory in their blackness, knowing that we have important work to do for ourselves and for this world. We want them to believe that unimagined miracles are in the wings preparing for an unprecedented entrance onto the main stage of human affairs: and we pray each one of them will be in the vanguard."

With Ossie & Ruby: In This Life Together, 1998

OSSIE DAVIS

"We want them to know that the essence of human history—the meaning of the existence—did come to tarry awhile in our home, in the bosom of one particular family;

that the glory of God and the cumulative light of all knowledge, the summing up of the entire human experience—civilization itself—shone at its brightest there. We want them
to know that, if only for one lifetime, under that one roof,
all meaning came to rest. Time ran its endless circle through
our living room; all space extended there. That our little
band, happy for the most part, but crying together too,
spent time at the center of Creation, right next to the throb-
bing heart of God Himself."

With Ossie & Ruby: In This Life Together, 1998

SINBAD

"My mother and father taught me everything: integrity, honesty, being responsible. My father said you can't be anything
unless you accept responsibility for all your failures. My
mother wanted me to have a tough hide but a tender heart."

Parade, September 11, 1994

RON DELLUMS

"True peace entails more than the absence of war. It requires
an unceasing effort to eliminate injustice, promote world
peace and create a compassionate society—this is the legacy
we must leave our children."

Address in celebration of his twenty years
of service in Congress, February 27, 1988

TONI MORRISON

"Children are resilient: and they take what they need from
the world and from anyone else they know."

Essence, December 1976

"It is hard raising children. Your children will try you every moment. You will not win all of the arguments. Be prepared to lose some of them, because if you win all of them your children will never grow up. And sometimes you must be willing to let them fall on their faces."

Essence, May 1995

BILL COSBY
"Whenever your kids are out of control, you can take comfort from the thought that even God's omnipotence did not extend to His kids. After creating heaven and earth, the oceans, and the entire animal kingdom, God created Adam and Eve. And the first thing He said was 'Don't.'"

"Human beings are the only creatures on earth that allow their children to come back home."

Fatherhood, 1986

QUINCY JONES
"My kids ... are all of mixed blood, but they choose to think of themselves as black, and they're proud of it—not because they don't want to be white but because they relate most deeply to the rich heritage of black culture, with all the heartache and all the joy that go along with it."

Playboy, July 1990

KENNETH B. CLARK
"Are children born with racial feeling? Or do they have to learn, first, what color they are and second, what color is best? ... Learning about races and racial differences, learning

one's own racial identity, learning which race is to be pre-
ferred and which rejected—all these are assimilated by the
child as part of the total pattern of ideas he acquires about
himself and the society in which he lives."

Prejudice and Your Child, 1955

DAVID DINKINS

"No matter how rich and powerful we become, we cannot be
satisfied when many children experience the sunset of opportunity at the dawn of their existence."

Vital Issues: Journal of African American Speeches, 1991

MARIAN WRIGHT EDELMAN

"We need to stop punishing children because we don't like
their parents."

"The question is not whether we can afford to invest in every
child; it is whether we can afford not to."

The Measure of Our Success, 1992

BERNICE JOHNSON REAGON

"When I work with young people, I tell them, don't hand
me anything with a missing step. A missing step is a hole
that will break your leg and can pull your whole project
down. I have no tolerance for people who skip steps; they're
dangerous to themselves, their work, and everything else. If
you want to be someplace else you have to start walking. Do
the steps—."

"Sweet Honey: A Cappella Activists,"
Ms., March/April 1993

MARIAN WRIGHT EDELMAN
"Tell our children they're not going to jive their way up the career ladder. They have to work their way up hard. There's no fast elevator to the top."

Ebony, August 1988

LORRAINE HANSBERRY
"Seem like God don't see fit to give the black man nothing but dreams—but He did give us children to make them dreams seem worthwhile."

A Raisin in the Sun, 1959

DENZEL WASHINGTON
"At the Boys & Girls Clubs, we have a saying: 'If you want to change the world, start by changing the life of a child.'"

"Positive influences that rain down on us in childhood. That's where we find our shape, and our confidence, and our strength. That's where we take root."

A Hand to Guide Me, 2006

MARTIN LUTHER KING JR.
"A hundred times I have been asked why we have allowed little children to march in demonstrations, to freeze and suffer in jails, to be exposed to bullets and dynamite. The questions imply that we have revealed a want of family feeling or recklessness toward family security. The answer is simple. Our children and our families are maimed a little every day of our lives. If we can end an incessant torture by a single climatic confrontation, the risks are acceptable. Moreover,

our family life will be born anew if we fight together. Other families may be fortunate enough to be able to protect their young from danger. Our families, as we have seen, are different. Oppression has again and again divided and splintered them. We are a people torn apart from era to era. It is logical, moral and psychologically constructive for us to resist oppression united as families. Out of this unity, out of the bond of fighting together, forges will come. The inner strength and integrity will make us whole again."

Address at Abbott House, Westchester County, New York,
October 29, 1965

3.

MOVERS AND SHAKERS: LEADERS AND HEROES

SHIRLEY CHISHOLM

"Women have a special contribution to make to help bring order out of chaos in our nation because they have special qualities of leadership which are greatly needed today. And these qualities are the patience, tolerance, and perseverance which have developed in many women because of suppression. And if we can add to these qualities a reservoir of information about the techniques of community action, we can indeed become effective harbingers for change."

Address at the Conference of
Women's Employment, 1970

MAYA ANGELOU

"The needs of society determine its ethics, and in the Black American ghettos the hero is that man who is offered only the crumbs from his country's table but by ingenuity and courage is able to take for himself a Lucullan feast."

I Know Why the Caged Bird Sings, 1969

MARIAN ANDERSON

"Leadership should be born out of the understanding of the needs of those who would be affected by it."

"There are many persons ready to do what is right because in their hearts they know it is right. But they hesitate, waiting for the other fellow to make the first move—and he, in turn, waits for you. The minute a person whose word means a great deal dares to take the open-hearted and courageous way, many others follow."

My Lord, What a Morning, 1956

DENZEL WASHINGTON
"Ordinary people accomplishing extraordinary things? Perhaps. But I'll go one better and suggest that we're all extraordinary in our own way, and that it's what we do with our extraordinariness that sets us apart and makes the difference."
A Hand to Guide Me, 2006

MICHELLE OBAMA
"When you've had some success, it's not enough to just kick back and enjoy it. You've got to reach back and pull someone else up too."
Essence, September 2010

GAYRAUD WILMORE
"Our greatest fighters for freedom were religious leaders."
Best Black Sermons, 1972

MARCUS GARVEY
"There has never been a Movement where the Leader has not suffered for the Cause, and not received the ingratitude of the people. I, like the rest, am prepared for the consequence."

"Men who are in earnest are not afraid of the consequences."
Philosophy and Opinions, 1923

MARVA COLLINS
"Readers are leaders. Thinkers succeed."
Marva's Way, 1986

JESSE JACKSON
"I watched Adam Powell lead a depressed people to high spirits
with intellectual savvy. Dr. King, with sheer power of his personality, intellect, and commitment, lift his people. Dr. Benjamin Mays take patience and mold and shape young minds.
John Johnson take a five-hundred-dollar loan from his mother
and build a publishing empire. Percy Sutton, with grace and
class, go into public service, then into business. I drew strength
from the shadows of these giants and tried to absorb into my
own being the highest and best they had to offer."
Ebony Man, December 1986

MATTHEW HENSON
"As I stood there at the top of the world and thought of the
hundreds of men who had lost their lives in the effort to
reach it [the North Pole], I felt profoundly grateful that I
had the honor of representing my race."
Ebony, November 1983

JOHN BROWN RUSSWURM
"The greatest stimulus ever presented to the man of color in
the United States has been the promotion of men of his race
to offices of great trust and responsibility."
Dispatch to John B. Latrobe, President,
Maryland Colonization Society, December 30, 1845

ANITA DEFRANTZ
"We need leadership that thinks about the future and en-
courages us to invest in ourselves."
American Visions, 1988

CORETTA SCOTT KING

"Women, in general, are not a part of the corruption of the past, so they can give a new kind of leadership, a new image for mankind."

In Search of Our Mothers' Gardens, 1983

DOROTHY HEIGHT

"I am grateful to have been in a time and place where I could be a part of what was needed."

Inscribed on the Congressional Medal of Honor, presented by President George W. Bush, December 2004

BILL COSBY

"We've got to examine who and what a hero is and how far we the fans go in putting these people on pedestals. They are not perfect, but then again, neither are we."

Playboy, December 1985

QUEEN LATIFAH

"Being considered a leader can be a hassle. Some people put you on a pedestal and don't let you be human. It's like they see themselves in you—they see their best self in you and they expect perfection from their best self . . . but I'm no saint. I can slip, just like anybody else."

Los Angeles Times, September 8, 1991

RON KARENGA
"None of our heroes fail because of progressive perfection.
They did as much as they could given the time and the
circumstances."
Speech at Yale University, New Haven, Connecticut 1967

ADAM CLAYTON POWELL JR.
"The people of the streets, the failures, the misfits, the de-
spised, the maimed, the beaten, the sightless and the voice-
less had made a captive of me. . . . Whenever they
commanded, I followed, but followed only to lead."
Adam by Adam, 1971

A. PHILIP RANDOLPH
"A leader of the masses must be free to obey and follow the
interests of the masses."
Speech at March on Washington,
Detroit, Michigan, September 26, 1942

ADAM CLAYTON POWELL JR.
"To demand these God-given rights is to seek black
power—what I call audacious power—the power to build
black institutions of splendid achievement."
Commencement Address, Howard University, May 28, 1966

JAMES BALDWIN
"Heroes can be found less in large things than in small ones,
less in public than in private."
Nobody Knows My Name, 1961

ANDREW YOUNG
"Democracy, to be effective, requires that leaders perform heroically."

A Way Out of No Way, 2008

SHIRLEY CHISHOLM
"Far too often we become cowards when faced with individuals who have strong leadership abilities, individuals who often do not want social revolution as much as they want personal power. Far too often we follow blindly—without questioning their motives—without examining their actions. We follow blindly because what they say they want to do sounds right. We follow because we are afraid that those around us will misunderstand our questions and put us down."

Speech in 1969, from *Boston Globe,* 2005

W. E. B. DuBois
"There are those who go down in the blood and dust of battle. They say ugly things to an ugly world. They spew the lukewarm fence straddlers out of their mouths, like God of old; they cry aloud and spare not; they shout from the housetops, and they make this world so damned uncomfortable with its nasty burden of evil that it tries to get good and does get better."

The Crisis, May 1914

CHARLAYNE HUNTER-GAULT
"When people at the top exercise aggressive leadership and will, even when they don't work miracles, they set a tone and create an atmosphere that make things happen."

In My Place, 1992

ANGELA DAVIS
"The work of the political activist inevitably involves a certain tension between the requirement that positions be taken on current issues as they arise and the desire that one's contribution will somehow survive the ravages of time."
Women, Culture and Politics, 1989

SHIRLEY CHISHOLM
"The Presidency is for white males. No one was ready to take a black woman seriously as a candidate. It was not time yet for a black to run, let alone a woman and certainly not for someone who was both. Someday . . . but not yet. Someday the country would be ready. . . . I ran because someone had to do it first. In this country everybody is supposed to be able to run for President. I ran because most people think the country is not ready for a black candidate, not ready for a woman candidate. Someday . . . it was time in 1972 to make someday come."
The Good Fight, 1973

ANGELA DAVIS
"Radical simply means grasping things at the root."
Address, Spellman College, June 5, 1987

LANI GUINIER
"Democracy in a heterogeneous society is incompatible with rule by a racial monopoly of any color."
The Tyranny of the Majority, 1994

"I am a democratic idealist who believes that politics need not be forever seen as I win, you lose, a dynamic in which some people are permanent monopoly winners and other are permanent excluded losers."

Press conference, Justice Department
Washington, D.C., June 4, 1994

CORNEL WEST
"We need leaders—neither saints nor sparkling TV personalities—who can situate themselves within a larger historical narrative of this country and our world, who can grasp the complex dynamics of our peoplehood and imagine a future grounded in the best of our past, yet who are attuned to the frightening obstacles that now perplex us."

Race Matters, 1993

KAREEM ABDUL-JABBAR
"I basically played on an idea, which is how close I could come to being at my best. I put some hard work into that, I had the good fortune to have been given talent, and I was lucky enough not to have gotten hurt. . . . There comes a time to give things up, to let things go. . . . But now it's time to let one life end and see what happens in my new life as a regular citizen. The sport goes on. People will find new heroes. And I'm flattered they'll be compared to me."

Kareem, 1990

"[Jesse Owens] owes the men who have come before him, the ones who helped him personally and many more who helped by standing up and not copping out when it counted. . . . He owes it to a lot of men, as yet unborn, who'll stand up in the future."

Blackthink, 1970

BARACK OBAMA
"What satisfies me . . . being useful to my family and the people who elected me, leaving behind a legacy that will make our children's lives more hopeful than our own."

"I think about America and those who built it. This nation's founders, who somehow rose above petty ambitions and narrow calculations to imagine a nation unfurling across a continent. And those like Lincoln and King, who ultimately laid down their lives in the service of perfecting an imperfect union. And all the faceless, nameless men and women, slaves and soldiers and tailors and butchers, constructing lives for themselves and their children and grandchildren, brick by brick, rail by rail, calloused hand by calloused hand, to fill in the landscape of our collected dreams.

"It is that process I wish to be a part of.

"My heart is filled with love for this country."

The Audacity of Hope, 2006

4.

AND STILL
I RISE:
OVERCOMING
OBSTACLES

FRANCES W. HARPER
"Oh, could slavery exist long if it did not sit on a commercial throne?"

Letter, Temple, Maine, October 20, 1854

JAMES W. C. PENNINGTON
"There is one sin that slavery committed against me which I can never forgive. It robbed me of my education. That injury is irreparable."

Fugitive Blacksmith, 1850

DAVID WALKER
"Treat us like men and we will be your friends."

Appeal in Four Articles, IV, 1829

HARRIET TUBMAN
"I was the conductor of the Underground Railroad for eight years, and I can say what most conductors can't say—I never ran my train off the track and I never lost a passenger."

Inscription, Harriet Tubman Memorial, Auburn, New York

"I freed a thousand slaves—I could have freed a thousand more if only they knew they were slaves."

circa 1865

PHILLIS WHEATLEY
"A hundred thousand new-born babies are annually added to the victims of slavery; twenty thousand lives are annually sacrificed on the plantations of the South. Such a sight

should send horror through the nerves of civilization and impel the heart of humanity to lofty deeds. So it might if men had not found out a fearful alchemy by which this blood can be transformed into gold. Instead of listening to the cry of agony, they listen to the ring of dollars and stoop to pick up the coin."

Address, Antislavery Society Convention,
New York City, May 13, 1857

RICHARD ALLEN

"A black man, although reduced to the most abject state human nature is capable of, short of real madness, can think, reflect and feel injuries, although it not be with the same degree of keen resentment and revenge that you who have been our great oppressors would manifest if reduced to the pitiable condition of a slave."

*The Life Experience and Gospel Labors of
the Right Reverend Richard Allen,* 1887

HENRY BIBB

"Among the good trades, I learned the art of running away to perfection. I made a regular business of it and never gave it up until I broke the bands of slavery."

Narrative of the Life and Adventures of Henry Bibb, 1849

"You may think hard of us for running away from slavery but as to myself, I have but one apology to make for it . . . that I did not start at an earlier period. I might have been free long before I was."

Letter to W. H. Gatewood (his former master), March 28, 1844

JAMES CONE

"Anger and humor are like the left and right arm. They complement each other. Anger empowers the poor to declare their uncompromising opposition to oppression, and humor prevents them from being consumed by their fury."

Martin and Malcolm in America, 1991

FREDERICK DOUGLASS

"To imagine that we shall ever be eradicated is absurd and ridiculous. We can be modified, changed, and assimilated, but never extinguished."

"The white man's happiness cannot be purchased by the black man's misery."

"The Destiny of Colored Americans,"
The North Star, November 16, 1849

"No man can point to any law in the U.S. by which slavery was originally established. Men first make slaves and then make laws."

"The price of liberty is eternal vigilance."

Address, Bethel Literary and Historical
Association, Washington, D.C., April 1889

PHILLIS WHEATLEY

"In every human Breast, God has implanted a Principle, which we call Love of Freedom; it is impatient of Oppression and pants for Deliverance; and by the Leave of our Modern Egyptians I will assert that the same Principle lives in us."

Letter to Samson Occom, February 11, 1774

AUDRE LORDE

"It is not our differences that divide us. It is our inability to recognize, accept, and celebrate those differences."

Sister Outsider, 1984

"You do not have to be me in order for us to fight alongside each other. I do not have to be you to recognize that our wars are the same. What we must do is commit ourselves to some future that can include each other."

Speech, "Learning from the 60's," February 1982

MARY CHURCH TERRELL

"Lynching is the aftermath of slavery."

North American Review, June 1904

NIKKI GIOVANNI

"The 60's are that period in which a generation went from consciousness to cynicism without passing through compassion."

Catalyst, Summer 1988

RITA DOVE

"Not that I'd want to forget being black, but I would love to walk through life without the anxiety of being prejudged and pigeonholed on the basis of race."

Callaloo, Spring 1991

STOKELY CARMICHAEL
"The act of registering to vote . . . marks the beginning of political modernization by broadening the base of participation. It also does something the existentialists talk about: it gives one a sense of being. The black man who goes to register is saying to the white man, No."
Black Power: The Politics of Liberation in America, 1967

ELDRIDGE CLEAVER
"The question of the Negro's place in America, which for a long time could actually be kicked around as a serious question, has been decisively resolved: he is here to stay."
Soul on Ice, 1968

"The enemies of black people have learned something from history . . . and they are discovering new ways to divide us faster than we are discovering new ways to unite."
Open Letter to Stokely Carmichael, 1968

AUGUST WILSON
"It's a testament to the resilience of the human spirit that despite the conditions we have known, despite all the horrors of slavery, despite the sometimes brutal mistreatment blacks have received in this country, we're still here, still managing through it all to find a way to live life with dignity and a certain amount of nobility."
The New York Times, April 15, 1990

"People kill me talking about niggers is lazy. Niggers is the most hard-working people in the world. Worked 300 years for free. And didn't take a lunch hour."

Two Trains Running, 1990

BENJAMIN BANNEKER

"The color of the skin is in no way connected with strength of the mind or intellectual powers."

"Presumption should never make us neglect that which appears easy to us, nor despair make us lose courage in the sight of difficulties."

Banneker's Almanac, 1796

RACHEL ROBINSON

"We engaged in a struggle that will be ongoing for generations, I fear. So the willingness to fight back and the psychological stamina and discipline to keep focused on basic goals is essential."

"The committed individual can find a way of making a difference."

I Dream a World, 1989

MELBA PATTILLO BEALS

"We began moving forward [toward the high school]. The eerie silence of that moment would forever be etched in my memory. All I could hear was my own heartbeat and the sounds of boots clicking on the stone.

"Everyone seemed to be moving in slow motion as I peered past the raised bayonets of the 101st soldiers. I walked on the concrete path toward the front door of the school, the same path the Arkansas National Guard had blocked us from days before. We approached the stairs, our feet moving in unison to the rhythm of the marching click-clack sound of the Screaming Eagles [soldiers of the U.S. Army 101st Airborne Division]. Step by step we climbed upward—where none of my people had ever walked before as students. We stepped up to the door of Central High School and crossed the threshold into that place where angry segregationist mobs had forbidden us to go."

"The task that remains is to cope with our interdependence—to see ourselves reflected in every other human being and to respect and honor our differences."

Warriors Don't Cry, 1994

ABBEY LINCOLN
"You really can't have paradise on top of someone else's misery."

Essence, April 1992

MARIAN ANDERSON
"As long as you keep a person down, some part of you has to be down there to hold him down, so that means you cannot soar as you otherwise might."

My Lord, What a Morning, 1956

MADAM C. J. WALKER
"Don't sit down and wait for the opportunities to come; you have to get up and make them."

Why the Company Succeeded,
1924 Yearbook and Almanac, 1924

ARTHUR ALFONSO SCHOMBURG
"Pride of race is the antidote to prejudice."
The Negro Digs Up His Past, 1925

WALTER WHITE
"The Negro must, without yielding, continue the grim struggle *for* integration and *against* segregation for his own physical, moral, and spiritual well-being and for that of white America and of the world at large."
The Black 100, by Columbus Salley, 1993

BENJAMIN HOOKS
"Let's fight on until justice runs down like water and righteousness as a mighty stream. Let's fight on until there is no downsizing, until there is no glass ceiling. Let's fight on until God shall gather the four winds of heaven: until the angel shall plant one foot on the sea and the other on dry land and declare that the time that has been will be no more. Fight on, until the lion shall lie down with the lamb. Fight on, until justice, righteousness, hope, equality and opportunity is the birthright of all Americans."
From a speech at the NAACP 100th Anniversary Convention in New York, July 2009

THURGOOD MARSHALL
"The legal system can force open doors, and sometimes even knock down walls, but it cannot build bridges. That job belongs to you and me. The country can't do it. Afro and white, rich and poor, educated and illiterate, our fates are bound together. We can run from each other, but we cannot

escape each other. We will only attain freedom if we learn to appreciate what is different, and muster the courage to discover what is fundamentally the same. American diversity offers so much richness and opportunity. Take a chance, won't you? Knock down the fences which divide. Tear down the walls that imprison you. Reach out. Freedom lies just on the other side. We shall have liberty for all."

From his acceptance speech for Liberty Medal,
Philadelphia, Pennsylvania, July 4, 1991

ROSA PARKS

"Four decades later I am still uncomfortable with the credit given to me for starting the bus boycott. Many people do not know the whole truth. I would like them to know I was not the only person involved. I was just one of many who fought for freedom. And many others around me began to want to fight for their rights as well."

Quiet Strength, 1994

A. PHILIP RANDOLPH

"Freedom is never given; it is won."

Keynote Address, Second National Negro Congress, 1937

"We are gathered here in the largest demonstration in the history of this nation. Let the nation and the world know the meaning of our numbers. We are not pressure groups, we are not an organization or a group of organizations, we are not a mob. We are the advance guard of a massive moral revolution for jobs and freedom."

Speech at the Lincoln Memorial,
March on Washington, September 26, 1942

"We want full citizenship with no reservations. We will accept nothing less. . . . This condition of freedom, equality, and democracy is not the gift of the gods. It is the task of men, yes, men, brave men, honest men, determined men."

> Keynote Address to the Policy Conference, March on
> Washington Movement, Detroit, September 26, 1942

MEDGAR EVERS
"I'm looking to be shot any time I step out of my car. . . . If I die, it will be in a good cause. I've been fighting for America just as much as the soldiers in Vietnam."

> *Before the Mayflower,* 1982

"The gifts of God . . . should be enjoyed by all citizens in Mississippi."

> *The Black 100,* 1993

FANNIE LOU HAMER
"White Americans today don't know what in the world to do because when they put us behind them, that's where they made their mistake. If they had put us in front they wouldn't have let us look back. But they put us behind them, and we watched every move they made."

> "The Special Plight of the Black Woman,"
> Address to the NAACP Legal Defense Fund
> Institute, New York, May 7, 1971

DERRICK BELL
"Black people are the magical faces at the bottom of society's well. Even the poorest whites, those who must live their

lives only a few levels above, gain their self-esteem by gazing down on us. Surely, they must know that their deliverance depends on letting down their ropes. Over time, many reach out, but most simply watch, mesmerized into maintaining their unspoken commitment to keeping us where we are, at whatever cost to them or to us."

"We yearn that our civil rights work will be crowned with success, but what we really want—want even more that success—is meaning. . . . This engagement and commitment is what black people have had to do since slavery: making something out of nothing. Carving out a humanity for oneself with absolutely nothing to help—save imagination, will, and unbelievable strength and courage. . . . It is a story less of success than survival through unrelenting struggle that leaves no room for giving up. We are all part of that history, and it is still unfolding."

Faces at the Bottom of the Well, 1987

"It appears that my worst fears have been realized: we have made progress in everything yet nothing has changed."

And We Are Not Saved, 1987

A. PHILIP RANDOLPH

"If Negroes secure their goals, immediate and remote, they must win them and to win them they must fight, sacrifice, suffer, go to jail and if need be, die for them. These rights will not be given. They must be taken."

On the 1963 March on Washington, from
Voices of Freedom, by Henry Hampton, 1990

RAY CHARLES

"Going blind. Sounds like a fate worse than death, doesn't it? Seems like something which would get a little kid down, make him afraid, and leave him half-crazy and sad. Well, I'm here to tell you that it didn't happen that way—at least not with me."

Brother Ray, 1978

JAMES EARL JONES

"I feel no flattery when people speak of my voice. I'm simply grateful that I found a way to work around my impairment. Once a stutterer, always a stutterer. If I get any credit for the way I sound, I accept it in the name of those of us who are impaired."

Voices and Silences, 1993

JACKIE ROBINSON

"The way I figured it, I was even with baseball and baseball with me. The game had done much for me and I had done much for it."

"I know that I am a black man in a white world. In 1972, in 1947, at my birth in 1919, I know that I never had it made."

I Never Had It Made, 1972

MARIAN WRIGHT EDELMAN

"Don't be afraid of falling. It doesn't matter how many times you fall down. All that matters is how many times you keep getting up."

Commencement Address,
Howard University, May 12, 1990

MYRLIE EVERS-WILLIAMS
"I have reached a point in my life where I understand the pain and the challenges, and my attitude is one of standing up with open arms to meet all of them."

I Dream a World, 1989

LOUIS FARRAKHAN
"There is no difficulty that man is faced with that a man does not have the ability to overcome, if he will summon the strength of his being against that obstacle in the pathway of his progress."

From an address, Symphony Hall,
Phoenix, Arizona, August 21, 1990

DOROTHY HEIGHT
"Greatness is not measured by what a man or woman can accomplish, but by the opposition he or she has to overcome to reach goals."

Inscribed on the Congressional Medal of Honor,
presented by President George W. Bush, December 2004

QUINCY JONES
"You don't have to let suffering become your experience in life, and you don't have to pass it along to other people just because it hurts. Learn from it. And grow from it. And teach your pain to sing."

Playboy, July 1990

QUEEN LATIFAH

"There is nothing wrong with being afraid. There is something wrong—definitely wrong—with being so afraid that you don't even try. I've always been more afraid of not trying something. If you try and fail, at least you know what you can't do, and it leaves you room to attempt something else and keep going for it until you find your niche. But if you never try, that is the biggest failure."

"I made decisions that I regret, and I took them as learning experiences."

Ladies First: Revelations of a Strong Black Women, 1999

EARVIN "MAGIC" JOHNSON

"Talent is never enough. With few exceptions, the best players are the hardest workers."

My Life, 1992

TERRY MCMILLAN

"I've always had a romantic notion about life, that it is meant to be good; that we have to find our own way; that God puts obstacles in our path to test us, to see what we're made of, to make us pay attention and take notice. If we pass this series of tests we will experience joy, love, a sense of accomplishment, spiritual enlightenment, perhaps even peace."

Essence, May 1995

ROSA PARKS
"I have learned throughout my life that what really matters is not whether we have problems but how we go through them."
Quiet Strength, 1994

COLIN POWELL
"Once you have experienced a failure or a disappointment, once you've analyzed it and gotten the lessons out of it—dump it."
Parade, August 13, 1989

"Get mad. Then get over it."
My American Journey, 1995

CONDOLEEZZA RICE
"I don't do life crisis. I really don't. Life is too short. Get over it. Move on."
University of Denver Magazine, Summer 2010

BERNICE JOHNSON REAGON
"Life's challenges are not supposed to paralyze you, they're supposed to help you discover who you are. They're the prod that moves you forward."
"Sweet Honey: A Cappella Activists,"
Ms., March/April 1993

WILMA RUDOLPH
"Believe me, the reward is not so great without the struggle."
Chicago Tribune, January 8, 1989

WALLY AMOS
"Every experience has a lesson. . . . You give things power over yourself and then they own you."

"It's your mental attitude that creates results in your life."
Parade, May 22, 1994

ANITA HILL
"It would have been more comfortable to remain silent. It took no initiative to inform anyone. But when I was asked by a representative of this committee to report my experience, I felt that I had to tell the truth. I could not keep silent."
Statement to the Senate Judiciary Committee,
October 11, 1991

CLARENCE THOMAS
"It takes a person with a mission to succeed."
Jet, November 26, 1984

"I am a product of hatred and love—hatred of the social and political structure which dominated the segregated, hate-filled city of my youth, and the love of some people— my mother, my grandparents, my neighbors and relatives— who said by their actions, you can make it, but you first must endure."

Commencement Speech at
Savannah State College,
June 9, 1985

"I was raised to survive under the totalitarianism of segregation, not only without the active assistance of government but with the active opposition. . . . Self sufficiency and spiritual and emotional security were our tools to carve out and secure freedom."

"Why Black Americans Should Look to Conservative Policies," Speech, August 1, 1987

"Mr. Chairman, in my forty-three years on this earth, I have been able with the help of others and with the help of God to defy poverty, avoid prison, overcome segregation, bigotry, racism, and obtain one of the finest educations available in this country. But I have not been able to overcome this process. This is worse than any obstacle or anything that I have ever faced. . . . I never asked to be nominated. It was an honor. Little did I know the price, but it is too high."

First Statement to the Senate Judiciary Committee, October 11, 1991

MAYA ANGELOU
"You may encounter many defeats, but you must not be defeated. In fact, it may be necessary to encounter the defeats, so you can know who you are, what you can rise from, how you can still come out of it."

Wouldn't Take Nothing for My Journey Now, 1994

RALPH J. BUNCHE
"There is no doubt that overwhelmingly the sympathy of the members of the UN, from all sections of the world and people of all colors, is for the American Negro in his heroic struggle

for justice. The eyes of the world are focused on this problem, on what happens in the United States. This has a tremendous effect on the United States' image abroad. I have always been confident that the Negro will win this struggle, but it is not the Negro, really, but the nation that must win it."

Negro Education, July 1935

HOWARD THURMAN

"Perhaps the authentic moral stature of a man is determined by his choice of weapons which he uses in his fight against the adversary. Of all weapons, love is the most deadly and devastating, and few there be who dare trust their fate in its hands."

The Oratory of Negro Leaders, 1969

"To love is to make of one's heart a swinging door."

Recapture the Spirit, 1973

JOHN HOPE FRANKLIN

"There is nothing inherently wrong with being aware of color as long as it is seen as making distinctions in a pleasant, superficial, and unimportant manner. It is only when character is attached to color, when ability is measured by color, when privilege is tied to color, and a whole galaxy of factors that spell the difference between success and failure in our society are tied to color—it is only when such considerations are attached to color that it becomes a deadly, dreadful, denigrating factor among us all. It is when it is such a factor that we have two nations, black and white, separate, hostile, unequal."

The Color Line: Legacy for the 21st Century, 1993

HENRY LOUIS GATES

"What I am calling humanism starts not with the possession of identity, but with the capacity to identity with. It asks what we have in common with others, while acknowledging the diversity among ourselves. It is about the promise of a shared humanity."

The New York Times, March 27, 1994

WALTER WHITE

"Intolerance can grow only in the soil of ignorance: from its branches grow all manner of obstacles to human progress."

Rope and Faggot, 1929

SAMUEL D. PROCTOR

"It does not matter where we are born, what kind of rearing we had, who our friends were, what kind of trouble we got into, how low we sank, or how far behind we fell. When we add it all up, we still have some options left, we still have some choices we can make."

Sermons from the Black Pulpit, 1984

ELIJAH MUHAMMAD

"Let us refrain from doing evil to each other, and let us love each other as brothers, as we are the same flesh and blood. . . . It is a fool who does not love himself and his people."

"No one of us will have to raise a sword. Not one gun would we need to fire. The great cannon that will be fired is our unity."

"We cannot be equal with the master until we own what the master owns. We cannot be equal with the master until we have the freedom the master enjoys. We cannot be equal with the master until we have the education that the master has. Then, we can say "Master, recognize us as your equal."
Message to the Blackman, 1965

ADRIAN PIPER
"I am the racists' nightmare, the obscenity of miscegenation. I am a reminder that segregation is impotent; a living embodiment of sexual desire that penetrates racial barriers and reproduces itself. I am the alien interloper, the invisible spy in the perfect disguise who slipped past the barricades in an unguarded moment. I am the reality of successful infiltration that ridicules the ideal of assimilation."
Funk Lessons Flying, Washington, D.C., February 1987

JILL NELSON
"From a distance, it's easy to start thinking that white folks run things because they're especially intelligent and hard-working. This, of course, is the image of themselves they like to project. Up close, most white folks, like most people, are mediocre. They've just rigged the system to privilege themselves and disadvantage everyone else."
Volunteer Slavery, 1993

SHARON EGRETTA SUTTON

"In my fifty years I have made two strenuous climbs into elite, white male domains—first as a classical musician, then as an architect. The combined reality of my race, gender and class is so tenacious—so insidious—that it has helped me to develop a stubborn resistance to the multiple layers of structural inequality."

Finding Our Voice in the Dominant Key, 1991

5.

DARE TO
DREAM:
FAITH, HOPE,
AND INSPIRATION

THELMA GOLDEN

"Going to museums as a child, it was clear that somebody put those things up. When it became clear to me what that job was, that was the job I wanted."

"Black Butterfly: Arts and Culture from Brooklyn to the Bay and Beyond," *Online* magazine, February 28, 2009

MARCUS GARVEY

"If you have no confidence in self you are twice defeated in the race for life. With confidence, you have won even before you have started."

"Lift up yourselves . . . take yourselves out of the mire and hitch your hope to the stars."

Philosophy and Opinions, 1923

NIKKI GIOVANNI

"I really don't think life is about the I-could-have-beens. . . . Life is only about the I-tried-to-do. I don't mind the failure but I can't imagine that I'd forgive myself if I didn't try."

Black Women Writers, 1984

JACKIE JOYNER-KERSEE

"I always say to myself, I will never forget what it took to get where I am. I see the struggle. I see the hard times. I would not abuse it by getting big headed and cocky. I always believe God gives it to you and God will take it away if he sees you cannot handle it."

Jet, July 10, 1989

LORRAINE HANSBERRY

"My people are poor. And they are tired. And they are determined."

"Though it be a thrilling and marvelous thing to be merely young and gifted in such times, it is doubly so, doubly dynamic—to be young, gifted and black. Look at the work that awaits you!"

To Be Young Gifted and Black, 1969

CORNEL WEST

"We must never give up hope. . . . I have hope for the next generation, though I think that they're up against a lot. But I believe in the ingenuity, the intelligence, the beauty, the laughter and the love that black people can give both themselves and others. And that is the raw stuff out of which any major movement for justice is made."

Emerge, October 1990

JUDITH JAMISON

"When you're looking at yourself in the mirror you have to remember that that image is only a part of you. The you inside . . . you realize how unique that is. Nobody can be you. Uniqueness needs to be celebrated. There's only one of you. You're totally and absolutely individual. . . . Self-definition is very important. You define who you are by the actions, by what you do with your life."

Dancing the Spirit: An Autobiography, 1993

OPRAH WINFREY

"What I have learned in my life and in my work is that the more I am able to be myself, the more it enables other people to be themselves."

"My race and my gender have been an issue for me. I have been blessed in knowing who I am, and I know it and intend to bear great fruit."

USA Today, February 10, 1987

"We will falter unless we know our purpose clearly. My purpose is to do my show every day and to raise the consciousness of people."

Wind Beneath My Wings, June 1989

"The difference between being famous and not is that people know your name."

I Dream a World, 1989

EARTHA KITT

"If you keep your soul clean, you'll wind up a much healthier person, and if you feel good about yourself you usually look it."

Essence, January 1993

THELMA GOLDEN

"One of the funniest experiences I had when I began working in the art world is that people always assumed I worked for Thelma Golden, not that I was Thelma Golden. This kind of dismissal that comes from just people's sense that they don't imagine you are who you are actually has been one of the most powerful and liberating things for me in my work."

The Black List Project, Internet Media, 2010

SUSAN TAYLOR
"Seeds of faith are always within us; sometimes it takes a crisis to nourish and encourage their growth."

"Our greatest problems in life come not so much from the situations we confront as from our doubts about our ability to handle them."

"Use missteps as stepping stones to deeper understanding and greater achievement."

Essence, August 1991

KIMORA LEE SIMMONS
"But you can't care too much about what people think of you. You have to establish your own set of core values and live by them, honor, respect, tenacity, intelligence and humor. Do your best, and live with the repercussions of your choices—good or bad."

People, June 10, 2008

GEORGE WASHINGTON CARVER
"How far you go in life depends on your being tender with the young, compassionate with the aged, sympathetic with the striving, and tolerant of the weak and strong. Because someday in life you will have been all of these."

circa 1920, from *George Washington Carver: In His Own Words,* 1987

ARTHUR ASHE

"Believe me, most people resist change, even when it promises to be for the better. But change will come, and if you acknowledge this simple but indisputable fact of life, and understand that you must adjust to all change, then you will have a head start."

Day of Grace: A Memoir, 1994 (letter to his daughter)

JEAN TOOMER

"Once a man has tasted creative action, then thereafter, no matter how safely he schools himself in patience, he is restive, acutely dissatisfied with anything else. He becomes as a lover to whom abstinence is intolerable."

The Lives of Jean Toomer, 1987

"Talk about it only enough to do it. Dream about it only enough to feel it. Think about it only enough to understand it. Contemplate it only enough to be it."

"We have many reformers, few transformers."

"We start with gifts. Merit comes from what we make of them."

"One may receive the information but miss the teaching."

"We learn the rope of life by untying the knots."

"Fear is a noose that binds until it strangles."

Essentials: Definitions and Aphorisms, 1931

JESSE OWENS
"The battles that count aren't the ones for gold medals. The struggles within yourself—the invisible, inevitable battles inside all of us—that's where it's at."

"One chance is all you need."

"Find the good. It's all around you. Find it, showcase it and you'll start believing in it."

Blackthink, 1970

RITA DOVE
"We tend to close off our souls and it just isn't cool to talk about it, to talk about having an interior life. If we don't acknowledge our own interior lives, we don't permit others to have them."

Washington Post, April 22, 1994

RON DELLUMS
"The pain of being a black elected official carrying progressive ideas, when people in the media would render you invisible with the flick of the pen. What's welled up inside me is 20 years of pain."

"I get up every day really humbled by the fact that there is so much that I don't know."

Los Angeles Times, April 11, 1993

LANGSTON HUGHES
"Hold fast to dreams/ For if dreams die/ Life is a broken-winged bird/ Life is a barren field/ Frozen with snow."

The Dream Keeper and Other Poems, 1932

CORNEL WEST

"Let us hope and pray that the vast intelligence, imagination, humor, and courage of Americans will not fail us. Either we learn a new language of empathy and compassion, or the fire this time will consume us."

Race Matters, 2001

"It takes courage to interrogate yourself. It takes courage to look in the mirror and see past your reflection to who you really are when you take off the mask. . . . It takes courage to ask—how did I become so well-adjusted to injustice? It takes courage to cut against the grain and become a nonconformist. It takes courage to wake up and stay awake instead of engaging in complacent slumber. It takes courage to shatter conformity and cowardice. The courage to love truth is one of the preconditions of thinking critically. Thinking for oneself is based on a particular kind of courage in which you hold truth, wisdom, honesty in high esteem. The reason you want to think for yourself is because you understand that people often are not telling you the truth. When you place a high value on the truth, you have to think for yourself. If you're unwilling to muster the courage to think critically, then someone will do the thinking for you, offering doublethink and doubletalk relief. People will apply a certain kind of pressure to push you into complacency and maybe even cowardice. It's not long before you rationalize. *This isn't really me. I don't think that way.*"

Hope on a Tightrope, 2008

CLAUDE BROWN

"Despite everything that Harlem did to our generation, I think it gave something to a few. It gave them a strength that couldn't be obtained anywhere else."

Manchild in the Promised Land, 1965

ROY WILKINS

"There will always be honorable black people to come back to fight another day. . . . The struggle of life is not won with one glorious moment . . . but a continual struggle in which you keep your dignity intact and your powers at work, over the long course of a lifetime . . . learn the lessons . . . to follow the paths of decency, and to have courage, because it is hard to do."

Standing Fast: The Autobiography of Roy Wilkins, 1982

FANNIE LOU HAMER

"I have the right to stay here. With all that my parents and grandparents gave to Mississippi, I have a right to stay here and fight for what they didn't get."

Fannie Lou Hamer, 1990

WILLIAM WELLS BROWN

"You may place the slave where you please; you may dry up to your utmost fountains of his feelings, the springs of his thought; you may yoke him to your labour, as an ox which liveth only to work, and workest only to live; you may put him under any process which, without destroying his value as a slave, will debase and crush him as a rational human being; you may do this, and the idea that he was born to be free will survive it all. It is allied to his hope of immortality;

it is the ethereal part of his nature, which oppression cannot reach; it is a torch lit up in his soul by the hand of Deity, and never meant to be extinguished by the hand of man."

Clotel, 1853

Condoleezza Rice

"If I could wish one thing and do it over, the thing that I would do, in spite of all the expectations of me and in spite of all the duties and responsibilities would be to take a little bit more time enjoying fulfilling them."

From the biography *Twice as Good,* by Marcus Mabry, 2007

Geraldine Moore

"No matter what their particular status, most Negroes doubtlessly feel that there must be many things worse than being a Negro in Birmingham, for there are some whose lives and achievements have proved without a doubt that a person can do almost anything he wants to do if his faith in God, in man, and in himself is strong enough. There are hundreds whose lives are exemplary of the eternal truth that our greatest strengths are often born of adversity."

Behind the Ebony Mask: What American Negroes Really Think, 1961

John Hope Franklin

"The test of an advanced society is not in how many millionaires it can produce, but in how many law-abiding, hard-working, highly respected, and self-respecting loyal citizens it can produce. The success of such a venture is a measure of the success of our national enterprise."

Mirror to America: The Autobiography of John Hope Franklin, 2005

EARL GRAVES
"Continue to build wealth by looking within. Look for opportunities to expand your businesses. Invest in the black community with your time and money. Patronize other black-owned businesses. Hire black people to work with you. Continue to form alliances and partnerships with other black business people. Encourage others to reduce their debts and increase their savings. Show them how. In all things, be a force for responsible decision-making within your community."

Vital Issues: Journal of African American Speeches,
Winter 2001–Spring 2002

MARGARET WALKER
"Let a new earth rise. Let another world be born. Let a bloody peace be written in the sky. Let a second generation full of courage issue forth; let a people loving freedom come to growth."

For My People, 1942

JOHNNETTA B. COLE
"You must have courage to take a position where you may not know all the answers but you have the fortitude to ask the right questions."

Essence, May 2010

WALTER FAUNTROY
"Don't be intimidated by anything: we have everything it takes to change America. Don't be blinded by prejudice, disheartened by the times, or discouraged by the system.

Face the system, challenge the system; confront it, correct it, change it. Don't let anything paralyze your mind, tie your hands or break your spirit. If you have a hard way to go, walk it by faith. If you face a mean problem, work with it until you work through it. If you have a misunderstanding, settle it. If you have a grudge, drop it. If you have a hatred or resentment, shake it off. If you have a high mountain, move it by faith or climb it by works. If you have a battle, fight it. If you have a handicap, rise above it! If you have a temptation, conquer it. If you have an evil, destroy it. If you have a challenge, face it. If you have trouble, take it. If you have a cross, bear it. If they knock you down, get up. If they push you against the ropes, come out swinging. If they laugh at you, keep smiling at them. If they talk about you, keep praying for them. If they hate you, keep loving them. And kill you, just rise again!"

Vital Issues: Journal of African American Speeches,
Spring 2000

BERNICE JOHNSON REAGON
"If you stay in the safety zone all the time, you'll never know about your strength, you'll never know yourself at your most brilliant."

"Sweet Honey: A Cappella Activists,"
Ms., March/April 1993

MAE C. JEMISON
"It's important not only for a little black girl growing up to know, yes, you can become an astronaut because there's Mae

Jamison. But it's important for older white males who sometimes make decisions on those careers of those black girls."

The New York Times, September 13, 1992

RUTH B. LOVE

"Characteristics of good and great people:

Know yourself and lead with your strengths.

Know what you believe in and what you stand for.

Create a vision for your future and pursue it with excellence.

Understand that thoughts and words are things. They are
powerful. Think good thoughts and speak affirmatively.

Make courage a good friend. Be willing to take some risks
and endure the consequences.

Surround yourself with positive people. Nothing dims your
light more than negativism.

Commit yourself to helping others. No matter what you accomplish, always reach back and bring someone along.

Be a perpetual student—continue to learn and to grow. This
life is not a solo performance. We all need people, we need
knowledge."

Vital Issues: Journal of African American Speeches,
Fall 2000

EDDIE MURPHY

"All inspiration is from a higher power . . . you hear voices,
everybody does. When you get older, you refer to it as
intuition."

US, January 1993

SISTER SOULJAH
"Developing your mind and your psyche will keep you in control of your own reality."

Right On!, June 1992

CORNEL WEST
"The major enemy of black survival in American has been and is neither oppression nor exploitation but rather the nihilistic threat—that is, loss of hope and absence of meaning. For as long as hope remains and meaning is preserved, the possibility of overcoming oppression stays alive."

Race Matters, 1993

SUSAN TAYLOR
"Life is a journey of self-discovery. If we're not growing, we're not living fully. Growth requires self-examination. It requires that we slow the pace, step back from our lives and assess where we are and where we want to go, that we create and live the plan that will take us there."

Essence, October 1992

BENJAMIN E. MAYS
"The tragedy in life does not lie in not reaching your goal. The tragedy lies in having no goal to reach. It isn't a calamity to die with dreams unfulfilled, but it is a calamity not to dream. . . . It is not a disgrace not to reach the stars, but it is a disgrace to have no stars to reach for. Not failure but low aim is a sin."

Best Black Sermons, 1972

A. Philip Randolph

"We must have faith that this society, divided by race and class, and subject to profound social pressure, can one day become a nation of equals."

"Mass social pressure in the form of marches and picketing will not only touch and arrest the attention of the powerful public officials but also the little man in the street."

Speech at the Lincoln Memorial,
March on Washington, September 26, 1942

Denzel Washington

"Keep open—to possibility, to opportunity, to wonder—or remain forever shut off to the encouraging outcomes that await us all. Change happens. The key is to keep reaching for that guiding hand and keep extending your own."

A Hand to Guide Me, 2006

Mary McLeod Bethune

"I leave you love . . . hope . . . the challenge of developing confidence in one another . . . a thirst for education . . . a respect for the uses of power . . . faith . . . racial dignity . . . a desire to live harmoniously with your fellow men . . . a responsibility to our young people."

"Last Will and Testament," *Ebony,* 1982

Yvonne Brathwaite Burke

"I'm willing to take a chance because I really believe I'm going to win. But you're not going to win unless you try."

I Dream a World, 1989

BEN CARSON

"Everybody has barriers and obstacles. If you look at them as containing fences that don't allow you to advance, then you're going to be a failure. If you look at them as hurdles that strengthen you each time you go over one, then you're going to be a success."

Parade, December 25, 1988

"Listen and learn from people who have already been where you want to go. Benefit from their mistakes instead of repeating them. Read good books . . . because they open up new worlds of understanding."

"We create our own destiny by the way we do things. We have to take advantage of opportunities and be responsible for our choices."

"Success in life revolves around recognizing and using our abilities our raw talent."

Gifted Hands, 1990

CAROLE GIST

"It's nice to be first at something. I like being the one to help lay the groundwork."

Jet, March 26, 1990

MALCOLM GLADWELL

"Practice isn't the thing you do once you're good. It's the thing that makes you good."

"People don't rise from nothing. . . . It is only by asking where they are *from* that you can unravel the logic behind who succeeds and who doesn't."

Outliers: The Story of Success, 2008

EARVIN "MAGIC" JOHNSON
"Don't let anyone tell you what you can't do. If you don't succeed let it be because of you. Don't blame it on other people."

My Life, 1992

MARIAN ANDERSON
"Prayer begins where human capacity ends. "

My Lord, What a Morning, 1956

MARY McLEOD BETHUNE
"For God so loved the world, that He gave His only begotten Son, that whosoever believeth in Him shall not perish, but have everlasting Life. With these words the scales fell from my eyes and the light came flooding in. My sense of inferiority, my fear of handicaps, dropped away. Whosoever, it said. No Jew or Gentile, no Catholic nor Protestant, no black nor white; just 'whosoever.' It meant that I, a humble Negro girl, had just as much chance as anybody in the sight of God. These words stored up a battery of faith and confidence and determination in my heart, which has not failed me to this day."

"Faith that Moved a Dump Heap,"
Who, The Magazine about People, June 1941

JESSE JACKSON
"As I look back on the struggles and triumphs of my mother and the long line of black men and women who survived slavery and segregation and armies of doubting Thomases, I am grateful to the Lord for letting me see the glory of the coming of a new day, and I am persuaded once again, that God and history are not through with us yet."

Ebony, December 1995

SISTER SOULJAH
"Loneliness does not discriminate."

No Disrespect, 1994

TONI MORRISON
"If you enjoy your own company, there is no loneliness."

Essence, May 1995

"You repossess your life when you can laugh at the things that try to destroy you."

Washington Post, October 10, 1993

ROSA PARKS
"When so many others, by the hundreds and thousands joined in, there was a kind of lifting of a burden from me individually. I could feel I was not alone."

LIFE, Spring 1988

JOHNNETTA B. COLE

"What you give ought to be in direct relationship to what you've received. If you are blessed with a great deal, then you have a lot of giving to do."

Dream the Boldest Dreams, 1997

GUION S. BLUFORD

"I am awed at man's ingenuity and what he can achieve. I recognized what a beautiful fragile planet we live on. Seeing earth from 170 miles in space is not like standing on earth and looking at the moon."

USA Today, February 1, 1983

"When you are flying in space you get a much broader perspective of the world that we live in, and I think you recognize very quickly that this planet we live on is a small planet and we have to share it together. You recognize the importance of our managing our resources as effectively as possible, as well as the importance of getting along together. We are all passengers on this planet earth."

Black Visions '90: Afro-Americans in Space Science, February 1990

6.

GUIDING OUR YOUTH: TEACHING LIFE LESSONS

MARIAN WRIGHT EDELMAN

"Education is a precondition to survival in America today."

The Measure of Our Success, 1993

CONDOLEEZZA RICE

"As an educated person, you have tools to change your circumstances for the better whenever you find them stifling and along the way to change the lives of others, too. But you have to believe—like many who had less reason to have faith in tomorrow but nonetheless did—that the locomotive of human progress is individual will. And then you have only to act on it, confident that you will succeed."

University of Alabama General Commencement, May 15, 1994

JOHNNETTA B. COLE

"An education that teaches you to understand something about the world has done only half of the assignment. The other half is to teach you to do something about making the world a better place."

"Education is the single most consistent and powerful instrument for the advancement of an individual and a people."

Dream the Boldest, 1997

CAMILLE COSBY

"Education empowers you: it places you in a position to verbally challenge people who are giving you a whole lot of nonsense."

"I just want to be an agent for change. I want to do my part in helping people to change their negative attitudes about us as a people. And hopefully, if we have any negative attitudes about ourselves, I want to help change those too."

American Visions, December-January 1995

TONY BROWN

"I learned early in life that all I was going to have was what I was willing to work for."

Fortune, November 4, 1991

"The black community has to shift from an obsession with racism to an obsession with education."

Mother Jones, March-April 1993

SINBAD

"Nobody owes you anything. But you can go out and take it. With education. Pick up a book and read. Learn your history and everybody else's too. And don't be scared to be yourself."

Parade, September 11,1994

GEORGE WASHINGTON CARVER

"Education is the key to unlock the golden door of freedom."

circa 1912

"I wanted to know the name of every stone and flower and insect and bird and beast. I wanted to know where it got its color, where it got its life—but there was no one to tell me."

American Life, November 1923

"There was never a time in my youth, no matter how dark and discouraging the days might be, when one resolve did not continually remain with me, and that was a determination to secure an education at any cost."

Up from Slavery, 1901

ANNA JULIA COOPER
"Let our girls feel that we expect something more of them than they merely look pretty and appear well in society. Teach them that there is a race with special needs which they and only they can help; that the world needs and is already asking for their trained, efficient forces."

A Voice from the South: By a Black Woman of the South, 1892

LENA HORNE
"You have to be taught to be second class, you're not born that way."

Lena, 1965

JOHNNETTA B. COLE
"If you educate a man, you educate a man. If you educate a woman, you educate a nation."

Dream the Boldest Dreams, 1997

MARVA COLLINS
"Children want and can learn. Provide them with the right environment, the right motivation, and the right material and children will demonstrate their natural ability to excel."

Address at Calvin College, January 1990

"A good teacher can always make a poor student good and a good student superior."

"We can pay teachers to teach, but how much do you really pay a teacher to care?"

Marva Collins' Way, 1990

Barbara Jordan
"Education remains the key to both economic and political empowerment."

Barbara Jordan, 1977

Beverly Johnson
"You have to be insightful. Prepare yourself for the transitions you will have to undertake in life."

Right On, May 1979

Frederick Douglass
"A little learning indeed may be a dangerous thing, but the want of learning is a calamity to any people."

Address, Colored High School Commencement,
Baltimore, Maryland, June 22, 1894

Charlotte L. Forten
"Tomorrow school commences and although the pleasure I shall feel in again seeing my beloved teacher, and in resuming my studies will be much saddened by recent events, yet they shall be fresh incentive to more earnest study, to aid me

in fitting myself for laboring in a holy cause, for enabling me to do much towards changing the condition of my oppressed and suffering people."

The Journal of Charlotte L. Forten, June 4, 1854

THURGOOD MARSHALL
"Instead of making us copy out stuff on the blackboard after school, when we misbehaved, our teacher sent us down into the basement to learn parts of the Constitution. I made my way through every paragraph."

Interview, 1989

KAREEM ABDUL-JABBAR
"More people have to start spending as much time in the library as they do on the basketball court. If they took the idea that they could escape poverty through education, I think it would make a more basic and long-lasting change in the way things happen. ... What we need are positive, realistic goals and the willingness to work."

Kareem, 1990

MALCOLM X
"I have often reflected upon the new vistas that reading opened to me. I knew right there in prison that reading had changed forever the course of my life. As I see it today, the ability to read awoke in me some long dormant craving to be mentally alive."

The Autobiography of Malcolm X, 1965

"Without education, you are not going anywhere in this world."

"Education is the passport to the future, for tomorrow belongs to those who prepare for it today."

Speech, Militant Labor Forum, May 29, 1964

RONALD McNAIR
"I thanked God that through a Black University, I had the chance to develop, the desire and the opportunity to do."

Choosing to Succeed, 1986

CARTER G. WOODSON
"For me, education means to inspire people to live more abundantly, to learn to begin with life as they find it and make it better."

The Miseducation of the Negro, 1931

JAMES BROWN
"You can't accomplish anything by blowing up, burning up, stealing and looting. Don't terrorize. Organize. Don't burn. Give kids a chance to learn. . . . The real answer to race problems in this country is education. . . . Be ready. Be qualified. Own something. Be somebody. That's Black Power."

Statement on national television during the riots in Washington, D.C., 1968 (after Martin Luther King's death)

BOOKER T. WASHINGTON

"There were some doubts ... about admitting me as a student. ... After hours had passed, the head teacher said to me, 'The adjoining recitation-room needs sweeping. Take the broom and sweep it.' It occurred to me at once that here was my chance. ... I swept the recitation-room three times and I dusted four times. ... When I was through I reported to the head teacher ... she went into the room and inspected the floor and closets; then she took her handkerchief and rubbed it on the woodwork about the walls. When she was unable to find one bit of dirt on the floor, or a particle of dust on any of the furniture, she quietly remarked, 'I guess you will do to enter this institution.' "

Up from Slavery, 1901

"Brains, property, and character for the Negro will settle the question of civil rights. ... Educate the black man, mentally and industrially, and there will be no doubt of his prosperity."

Speech, Madison, Wisconsin, July 16, 1884

DAVID WALKER

"The bare name of educating the coloured people, scares our cruel oppressors almost to death."

David Walker's Appeal, 1829

W. E. B. DuBois

"The South believed an educated Negro to be a dangerous Negro. And the South was not wholly wrong: for education among all kinds of man always has had, and always will have, an element of danger and revolution, or dissatisfaction and discontent."

The Souls of Black Folk, 1903

JUDITH JAMISON
"A lot of young people I meet do not know what they want to do with the rest of their lives, while it's getting later and they're under pressure to make a decision. It's for them not to worry, but to be well prepared, open and educated. Learn as much as you can about everything. It's hard to tell young people to be patient, but that's what they need to do."

Dancing Spirit, 1993

REGINALD LEWIS
"It is all too little when we consider the day-to-day drama being inflicted upon many of our children who are of African or Hispanic descent and who are not yet fully included in the American dream.

"By working in this field in the future, I believe I am working for all Americans, because I truly believe that our society is highly vulnerable unless we join together in seeing this not as a particular problem of any one ethnic group, but as something that the nation must address as part of its own spirit of renewal."

Statement made several days before his death, January 1993, in *Why Should White Guys Have All the Fun?,* 2005

VANESSA WILLIAMS
"When I speak to groups of troubled teens, I tell them the story of my life. This is what happened to me, this is how I fought through it. What made me strong was believing in myself. If you believe in yourself you can endure anything."
Fanfare, July 10, 1994

GEORGE FOREMAN
"Everybody wants to be somebody. The thing you have to do is give them confidence they can. You have to give a kid a dream."
On Coaching Young Kids, 1989

"I know from experience that the marriage of mind and body makes the sum more powerful that the individual parts."
By George, 1995

JACKIE JOYNER-KERSEE
"She [her mother] taught me the importance of self-reliance, self-respect, and self-discipline. . . . She instilled in me to never take anything for granted, because life is a precious gift and the gift of life shouldn't be misused, but treasured."
Ebony, May 1993

PAUL ROBESON
"To be free—to walk the good American earth as equal citizens, to live without fear, to enjoy the fruits of our toil, to give our children every opportunity in life—that dream

which we have held so long in our hearts is today the destiny that we hold in our hands."

"The patter of their feet as they walk through Jim Crow barriers to attend school is the thunder of the marching men of Joshua, and the world rocks beneath their tread."

Here I Stand, 1988

ANN PLATO

"It is owing to the preservation of books, that we are led to embrace their contents. Oral instructions can benefit but one age and one set of hearers: but these silent teachers address all ages and all nations. They may sleep for a while and be neglected; but whenever the desire for information springs up in the human breast, there they are with mild wisdom ready to instruct and please us."

Education, 1841

MILES DAVIS

"When kids don't learn about their own heritage in school, they just don't care about school. . . . But you won't see it in the history books unless we get the power to write our own history and tell our story ourselves. Nobody else is going to do it for us and do it like it is supposed to be done."

Miles, 1989

CARTER G. WOODSON

"Negroes have and always have had their ideas about the nature of the universe, time and space, about appearance and reality, and about freedom and necessity. The effort of the

Negro to interpret man's relation to the universe shows just as much intelligence as we find in the philosophy of the Greeks. There were many Africans who were as wise as Socrates."

The Mis-Education of the Negro, 1931

MARY MCLEOD BETHUNE
"When they learn the fairy tales of mythical kings and queens, we must let them hear of the pharaohs and African kings and the brilliant pageantry of the Valley of the Nile; when they learn of Caesar and his legion, we must teach them of Hannibal and his Africans; when they learn of Shakespeare and Goethe, we must teach them of Pushkin and Dumas. . . . Whatever the white man has done, we have done, and often even better."

Journal of Negro History, January 1938

W. E. B. DuBois
"As a boy I knew little of Africa save legends and some music in my family. The books which we studied in the public schools had almost no information about Africa."

Speech given to the All-African People's Conference, 1958

RICHARD WRIGHT
"We had own our civilization in Africa before we were captured and carried off to this land. . . . We smelted iron, danced, made music, and recited folk poems; we sculptured, worked in glass, spun cotton and wool, wove baskets and cloth; we invented a medium of exchange, mined silver and gold, made pottery, we fashioned tools and utensils of

brass, bronze, ivory, quartz, and granite; we had our literature, our own systems of law, religion, medicine, science, and education."

12 Million Black Voices, 1941

MELBA PATTILLO BEALS
"If my Central High School Experience taught me one lesson, it is that we are not separate. The effort to separate ourselves whether by race, color, religion, or status is as costly to the separator as to those who would be separated. . . . The task that remains is to cope with our interdependence—to see ourselves reflected in every other human being and respect and honor our differences."

Warriors Don't Cry, 1994

KELLY MILLER
"The Negro college must furnish stimulus to hesitant Negro scholarship, garner, treasure and nourish group tradition, enlighten both races with a sense of the cultural worth and achievement of the constituency it represents, and supply the cultural guidance of the race."

The New Negro, 1925

J. SAUNDERS REDDING
"The final test of Afro-American studies will be the extent to which they rid the minds of whites and blacks alike of false learning and the extent to which they promote for blacks and whites alike a completely rewarding participation in American life."

The American Scholar, 1969

7.

HONORING OUR HERITAGE: WORDS OF WISDOM

MARIAN WRIGHT EDELMAN

"Don't assume the door is closed. Push on it."

"Don't confuse wealth or fame with character."
Commencement address, Howard University,
May 12, 1990

ROGER WILKINS

"The only thing I absolutely know about the future is that if
we fail to strike blows now, we cast forward no sparks to
light the way for others who will continue our struggle."
Movements, November 1989

MICHELLE OBAMA

"If you want a life free from drama, then you can't hang
around with people who thrive on drama."
Graduation Address, Academies of Anacostia,
Washington, D.C., 2010

MUHAMMAD ALI

"I don't have to be what you want me to be, I'm free to be
who I want to be."
The New York Times, October 25, 1964

"The man who views the world at 50 the same as he did at
20 has wasted 30 years of his life."
Playboy, November 1975

JOHN H. JOHNSON

"There is no balance in the life of money. You either have too much or too little. When you don't have it, you run like the devil to get it. When you do have it, you run like the devil to keep it."

Succeeding Against the Odds, 1989

"Wealth is really what you own and control, not how much you have in your pockets."

The Crisis, March 1986

A. PHILIP RANDOLPH

"No organization can do everything. Every organization can do something, and each organization is charged with the social responsibility to do that which it can and is built to do."

Speech, March on Washington Movement, Detroit, Michigan, September 26, 1942

ALICE WALKER

"There's a little voice that's always trying to tell you what is really right. To hear it, you need silence, which is hard to come by. This is the noisiest culture, and that accounts for a lot of mayhem. Some people have no idea there's a voice."

"Don't sit on your feelings, listen to them and be brave ... there's nothing left to lose. You might as well feel what you feel."

USA Weekend, January 19-21, 1996

BARBARA JORDAN

"What the people want is very simple. They want an America as good as its promise."

"The stakes . . . are too high for government to be a spectator sport."
  Commencement Address, Harvard University, June 16, 1977

NIKKI GIOVANNI

"It's foolish to determine what your life will be before you've even had a chance to live it."
Black Women Writers, 1984

ALEX HALEY

"The griots symbolize how all human ancestry goes back to some place, and some time, where there was no writing. Then, the memories and the mouths of ancient elders was the only way that early histories of government passed along . . . for all of us today to know who we are."
Ebony, August 1986

"I acknowledge immense debt to the griots of Africa—where today it is rightly said that when a griot dies, it as if a library has burned to the ground."
Roots, 1976

"Reunions are the conveyor belts of our individual histories. They affirm the thread of continuity, establish pride in self and kin, and transmit a family's awareness of itself, from the youngest to the oldest. Reunions are a means of communicating with our living kin and that in turn is testament to our heritage. Reunions are nothing less than a family's roots brought to the surface."

Ebony, August 1986

ROBERTA FLACK
"To live is to suffer: to survive is to find some meaning in the suffering."

Essence, February 1989

JOHNNETTA B. COLE
"It is best to leave while people still want us to stay."

"There is an important difference between what we need and what we want. Therein can lie the distinction between necessity and gluttony."

"Hoarding a good idea is the best way to lose it."

"Some of the very best ideas begin in our hearts. Then we can send them to our heads for a kind of intellectual affirmation."

"Learning to live with shortcomings may be the easiest way to shortchange yourself."

Dream the Boldest Dreams, 1997

SAMMY DAVIS JR.
"My religion is my religion. My people are my people. . . . My people are first. I happen to be a Black Jew. I am first Black and the religion I have chosen is Judaism."

"Sammy Davis Jr.: The World's Greatest Entertainer," *Ebony,* July 1990

RALPH ELLISON

"I am not ashamed of my grandparents for having been slaves. I am only ashamed of myself for having at one time been ashamed."

Invisible Man, 1952

ALICE WALKER

"To acknowledge our ancestors means we are aware that we did not make ourselves, that the line stretches all the way back, perhaps to God; or to Gods. We remember because it is an easy thing to forget; that we are not the first to suffer, rebel, fight, love and die. The grace with which we embrace life, in spite of the pain, the sorrows, is always a measure of what has gone before."

Revolutionary Petunias, 1970

DICK GREGORY

"When the white Christian missionaries went to Africa, the white folks had the Bible and the natives had the land. When the missionaries pulled out, they had the land and the natives had the Bible."

Black Manifesto: Religion, Racism, and Reparations, 1960

ELDRIDGE CLEAVER

"You don't have to teach people to be human. You have to teach them how to stop being inhuman."

Conversations with Eldridge Cleaver, 1970

QUEEN LATIFAH

"Find power. Find the queen who lives inside of you, embrace her, nourish her, praise her, hold her accountable, and love her. Become her."

Ladies First: Revelations of a Strong Black Women, 1999

BENJAMIN E. MAYS

"Every man and woman is born into the world to do something unique and something distinctive and if he or she does not do it, it will never be done."

Best Black Sermons, 1972

SISTER SOULJAH

"I have to teach, pass on information, communicate, fulfill my responsibility to serve and lift my community. Some people accept their responsibility, some people reject it, and some people pretend that they don't even know it exists."

Playboy, October 1992

JACKIE ROBINSON

"The many of us who attain what we may and forget those who help us along the line—we've got to remember that there are so many others to pull along the way. The farther we go, the farther we all go."

Baseball Has Done It, 1964

DENZEL WASHINGTON

"The real story, the universal story, is that we all stand upon another set of shoulders. We are, all of us, the sum of our influences. We've all been taken by the hand and led to a better, more purposeful place."

A Hand to Guide Me, 2006

ARTHUR ALFONSO SCHOMBURG
"History must restore what slavery took away, for it is the social damage of slavery that the present generation must repair and offset."

"The American Negro must remake his past in order to make his future."

The Negro Digs Up His Past, 1925

MAYA ANGELOU
"Knowing our legacy—undistorted by others and documented by those who lived it—correctly aligns you and me and our children in the continuing struggle to fully claim our dignity in all areas of life."

Africana Heritage, 2010

JAMES BALDWIN
"Know whence you came. If you know whence you came, there is really no limit to where you can go."

Fire Next Time, 1962

ALTHEA GIBSON
"No matter what accomplishments you make, someone helps you."

TIME, August 26, 1957

RON DELLUMS
"In order to deal more effectively with current crisis and future options, we need to have a better understanding of the reason for past failures and limited successes, so as to avoid the former and improve on the latter."
Vital Issues: Journal of African American Speeches, 1991

ADAM CLAYTON POWELL JR.
"There is no future for a people who deny their past."
Marching Blacks, Collection of Essays, 1945

"Freedom is an internal achievement rather than an external adjustment."

"Black Power is black responsibility."
Keep the Faith, Baby, 1967

ALTHEA GIBSON
"Most of us who aspire to be tops in our fields don't consider the amount of work required to stay tops."
So Much to Live For, 1968

MALCOLM GLADWELL
"To build a better world we need to replace the patchwork of lucky breaks and arbitrary advantages today that determine success—the fortunate birth dates and the happy accidents of history—with a society that provides opportunities for all."
Outliers: The Story of Success, 2008

MARIAN WRIGHT EDELMAN
"In life the test and consequences come before the lessons."
Commencement Address, Howard University, May 12, 1990

LEONTYNE PRICE
"The ultimate of being successful is the luxury of giving yourself the time to do what you want to do."
Interview, *Newsday,* February 1, 1976

JAMES BALDWIN
"Anyone who has struggled with poverty knows how extremely expensive it is to be poor."
"Fifth Ave. Uptown," *Esquire,* July 1960

ANDREW YOUNG
"I make people think. I make them mad. I make them argue with each other and me, and I deny them the opportunity to be uninvolved in what's going on in the world."

"I won't let people be neutral."
Washington Post, July 21, 1978

DENZEL WASHINGTON
"Receive your gifts with open arms, but don't wear them on your sleeve."
A Hand to Guide Me, 2006

BEN VEREEN
"If you don't love yourself, you have nothing to hold on to."
Washington Post, July 29, 1990

OCTAVIA BUTLER
"Ignorance is expensive."

Essence, May 1989

JACKIE "MOMS" MABLEY
"There ain't nothing' an ol' man can do but bring me a message from a young one."

Mom's best-known line said at many
of her comedy appearances

"Mr. Sullivan didn't want to give me but four minutes. Honey, it take Moms four minutes just to get out on stage."

Newsday, April 6, 1967

ADRIAN PIPER
"Change is intrinsically painful."

Arts Magazine, March 1991

SADIE AND BESSIE DELANY
"Well, we didn't order any credit cards! We don't spend what we don't have. . . . Imagine a bank sending credit cards to two ladies over a hundred years old!"

Having Our Say: The Delany Sisters' First 100 Years, 1993

MALCOLM GLADWELL
"The key to good decision making is not knowledge. It is understanding. We are swimming in the former. We are desperately lacking in the latter."

Blink: The Power of Thinking without Thinking, 2007

"It is not how much money we make that ultimately makes us happy between nine and five. It's whether our work fulfills us."

Outliers: The Story of Success, 2008

"The tipping point is that magical moment when an idea, trend, or social behavior crosses a threshold, tips and spreads like wildfire."

The Tipping Point, 2002

BERRY GORDY JR.
"You can read 25 positive things about yourself and feel great, and then you hear one negative thing that's a lie, and it bothers the hell out of you."

Los Angeles Times, December 1, 1994

GREGORY HINES
"Luck is opportunity meeting up with preparation, so you must prepare yourself to be lucky."

Parade, May 31, 1992

LENA HORNE
"It's not the load that breaks you down, it's the way you carry it."

Lena, 1965

BIOGRAPHICAL
BRIEFS

(in alphabetical order by last name)

Abdul-Jabbar, Kareem (1947–   ) He was more than seven feet tall while still in high school and went on to lead his UCLA team to three NCAA championships. His spectacular professional basketball playing led the L.A. Lakers to five NBA championships. He retired after a record-breaking twenty-five-year career.

Ali, Muhammad (1942–   ) Three-time world heavyweight champion and considered the greatest boxer in history.

Allen, Debbie (1950–   ) Dancer, actress, choreographer, and producer-director of film and television, most notably the sitcom *A Different World*

Allen, Richard (1760–1831) The founder and first bishop of the African Methodist Episcopal Church, the oldest Afro-American religious denomination in America. He was motivated by white congregants' forcing blacks to a segregated section for worship and prayer.

Amos, Wally (1937–   ) Business entrepreneur and founder of the Famous Amos Chocolate Cookie Corp. He became interested in cooking and wanted to improve on an aunt's chocolate chip cookies recipe.

Anderson, Marian (1902–1993) The first African American to be named a permanent member of the Metropolitan Opera Company and who notably performed at the White House.

Angelou, Maya (1926–   ) Writer, poet, and actress whose bestselling autobiography launched a prolific career as a writer and spokesperson on African-American life.

Armstrong, Louis "Satchmo" (1900–1971) A jazz artist with the trumpet who achieved worldwide popularity and was a vital musical force.

Ashe, Arthur (1943–1993) The first black man to reach the top ranks of international tennis. After retirement, he established credentials as a businessman, champion of just causes, and author of a three-volume definitive history of the black athlete.

Bailey, Pearl (1918–1990) Best known for her easygoing singing style, starring on Broadway, television, and in films. Later in life she became a spokesperson for diabetes and wrote several books, including an outstanding cookbook.

Baker, Josephine (1906–1975) She began performing at age thirteen and became an international star in France, celebrated for her provocative costumes and dance routines.

Baldwin, James (1924–1987) One of the most widely quoted contemporary black writers, with a broad range of literary output, including novels, plays, magazine articles, and essays.

Banneker, Benjamin (1731–1806) Self-taught, he became a naturalist, astronomer, inventor, poet, and early American scientific and mathematical genius. He was best known as a member of the survey team that designed the city plan for Washington, D.C.

Baraka, Amiri (1934–   ) The talent of this poet, novelist, and dramatist emerged during the 1960s with his biting-edge style and critical content. Baraka, formerly LeRoi Jones, is the author of more than twenty volumes and the leader of the Black Arts Movement.

Beals, Melba Pattillo (1941–   ) One of the nine teenagers chosen to integrate Central High School in Little Rock, Arkansas, in 1957. She earned a master's degree in journalism from Columbia University and began writing in newspapers and magazines. She is the chair of the Communications Department at Dominican University College in California.

Bearden, Romare (1911–1988) An artist and writer who gained notoriety during the height of the Harlem Renaissance as a creator of modern collages depicting the changing currents of twentieth-century black life.

Bell, Derrick (1930–   ) Activist, scholar, and author, he was a tenured professor at Harvard University Law School but was dismissed for refusing to end a leave of absence until a minority woman was appointed to the faculty.

Berry, Halle (1968–   ) A former model and first runner-up for the Miss USA pageant, she has appeared in numerous films and had a lead role in a television miniseries. She won the Academy Award for Best Actress for her role in *Monster's Ball*.

Berry, Mary Frances (1938–   ) An educator who held faculty and administrative positions at several universities, she is a noted historian and author of works contributing to social thought.

Bethune, Mary McLeod (1875–1955) Nationally recognized for her political, educational, and humanitarian achievements, she founded the National Council of Negro Women and established the Bethune-Cookman College.

Bibb, Henry (1815–1854) A fugitive slave, he settled in Canada where he founded a weekly publication and established a 1,300-acre haven for escaped slaves.

Bluford, Guion S. (1942–   ) As a pilot in the U.S. Air Force, he had his first space mission aboard *Challenger* and was a mission specialist aboard America's first Spacelab mission.

Brown, Claude (1934–2003) A lawyer who as a young man lived in a world of crime, gang wars, drugs, and reform schools, which he describes in his classic autobiography *Manchild in the Promised Land*.

Brown, H. Rap (1943–   ) Prominent among the Afro-American radicals in the 1960s, he became the head of the Student Non-Violent Coordinating Committee.

Brown, James (1934–2006) Hailed as the "Godfather of Soul" in the late 50s, he was a singer of gospel and rhythm and blues.

Brown, Tony (1933–   ) For more than twenty years the producer of his own television show, he is known as a writer who expresses his views on black pride.

Brown, William Wells (1815–1884) An ex-slave, abolitionist, and self-taught writer, he wrote more than sixteen volumes and penned the first Afro-American novel and play.

Bunche, Ralph J. (1904–1971) Diplomat, Phi Beta Kappa, and Ph.D. from Harvard, he joined the State Department and participated in the planning conferences for the formation of the United Nations. He was instrumental in the resolution of the post–World War II conflict in the Middle East and was awarded the Nobel Peace Prize.

Burke, Yvonne Brathwaite (1932–) With a law degree from the University of Southern California, she was the first African-American woman from California elected to the U.S. House of Representatives. After serving three terms, she became a specialist in public finance.

Butler, Octavia (1947–2006) The most prominent African-American science-fiction writer, she gained fame as a female pioneer in a white male domain.

Campbell, Bebe Moore (1950–2006) A journalist and author, she established herself as an important writer of nonfiction and contemporary fiction.

Carmichael, Stokely (1941–) As the head of the Student Nonviolent Coordinating Committee (SNCC), he first used the Black Power slogan to describe grassroots efforts at political and economic empowerment.

Carson, Ben (1957–) After being identified as a failure in school, he turned his life around, completed medical school, and became the director of Pediatric Neurosurgery at the Johns Hopkins Hospital. He is a medical pioneer in complicated brain surgery.

Carver, George Washington (1864–1943) An inventor born of slave parents, he received a master's degree in science. He was known as the "Wizard of Tuskegee" because of his work developing products from the peanut plant.

Catlett, Elizabeth (1919–) A prominent black artist for fifty years, she is acclaimed for her figurative sculptures and lithographs.

Charles, Ray (1933–2004) Blind since the age of seven, he became a legend in blues, jazz, soul, country, and pop as a vocalist accompanying himself on the piano. He was inducted into the Rock and Roll Hall of Fame.

Chisholm, Shirley (1924–2005) Educated at Columbia University, she became a teacher and later was the first black woman elected to Congress. She was the first woman to actively run as a U.S. presidential candidate.

Clark, Kenneth B. (1914–2005) At the dawn of the Harlem Renaissance, he attended Howard University and received his Ph.D. from Columbia University. He conducted studies and experiments using dolls to determine the psychological effect of institutional racism on black children, which profoundly affected the outcome of the landmark *Brown v. Board of Education* ruling on school segregation.

Cleage, Pearl (1948–) Educator, playwright, and bestselling contemporary novelist, she also writes about social issues and criticisms.

Cleaver, Eldridge (1935–1998) He began writing while incarcerated in various California prisons. After being paroled, he became minister of information for the Black Panthers and published the famous *Soul on Ice.*

Cole, Johnnetta B. (1936–) She attended Fisk University and Oberlin College and received her M.A. and Ph.D. in anthropology from Northwestern University. She became the first African-American woman to serve as president of Spelman College in Atlanta, Georgia.

Collins, Marva (1936–) Former public school teacher, she is the founder of Westside Preparatory School and National Teacher Training Institute in Chicago, promoting a philosophy of learning featuring self-discipline, the value of hard work, and self-esteem.

Coltrane, John (1926–1967) A musician playing the alto and tenor saxophone, he recorded prolifically during his short and controversial life, struggling with addiction. His works continued to be reissued because of his long solos playing several notes at once and improvisations based on scales rather than chords.

Cone, James (1925–) A leading theologian and author of important works on liberation theology, he focuses on the reappraisal of Christianity from the perspective of the oppressed black community.

Cooper, Anna Julia (1858–1964) An educator born of a slave mother, she studied at Columbia and the Sorbonne and was active in the women's and Pan-African movements.

Cosby, Bill (1937–) A comedian, actor, writer, recording artist, and businessman, he has been deemed one of the funniest comedians in America. He starred in an early television series, for which he won three Emmy Awards. His later television series extolled the joys and challenges of black marriage and family life.

Cosby, Camille (1945–   ) The indispensable wife and partner of Bill Cosby, she has made a major contribution as a philanthropist and educator.

Davis, Angela (1944–   ) Currently a teacher in higher education and political activist, she studied abroad and became one of the few women active with the Black Panthers, and was once on the FBI's "Most Wanted" list.

Davis, Miles (1926–1991) Trumpet player, composer, and bandleader, this jazz innovator was active for more than four decades, inspiring many other jazz greats.

Davis, Ossie (1917–2005) Actor, director, and playwright, he wrote *Purlie Victorious,* a play that was adapted for film. He performed in numerous film, stage, and television roles. As a pioneer, he dedicated time to create better opportunities for Afro-Americans in the theater and in films.

Davis, Sammy, Jr. (1925–1990) Making his stage debut at the age of three working with his father and uncle, he eventually became one of the world's greatest entertainers, famous for his acting, singing, dancing, and impersonations.

Dee, Ruby (1924–   ) Actress, civil rights activist, and writer, she was married for more than fifty years to Ossie Davis. She is known for her high-profile work in theater, television, and films.

DeFrantz, Anita (1952–   ) She became involved in organized sports in college and competed in the Olympic Games, where her team won a bronze medal in rowing. She was the first American woman and first African American to serve on the International Olympic Committee.

Delany, Sarah (Sadie) (1889–1999) and **Bessie** (1891–1995) These two sisters were born into a family that had risen within decades from slavery to prominence. Sarah became an educator, while Bessie was a doctor of dental surgery. They were prominent figures during the Harlem Renaissance and their autobiography, *Having Our Say,* became a bestseller, a Broadway play, and a television film.

Dellums, Ron (1935–   ) He received his master's in social work from the University of California, Berkeley, and became an active social worker. He was the mayor of Oakland, California, and was elected to thirteen terms as a

U.S. congressman, serving as the first black chairman of the House Armed Services Committee. He is outspoken about issues related to the military, race, and gender.

Dinkins, David (1927–) A New York politician who held several political offices, including Manhattan borough president, before becoming the first black mayor of New York City.

Douglass, Frederick (1817–1895) A self-educated ex-slave, abolitionist, journalist, orator, and diplomat, he used his exceptional oratory skills to advocate for the abolition of slavery and the rights of women to vote.

Dove, Rita (1952–) Author of a novel, a collection of short stories, and volumes of poetry, including *Thomas and Beulah,* which was awarded the Pulitzer Prize. She was selected as poet laureate to the Library of Congress.

DuBois, W. E. B. (1868–1963) Historian, scholar, educator, and sociologist, he was the first Afro-American to receive a Ph.D. from Harvard University and the founding member of the NAACP. He was the author of many books analyzing and commenting on the status of blacks in America.

Edelman, Marian Wright (1939–) A graduate of Yale Law School and active in the civil rights movement in the 1960s, she headed the Legal Defense and Education Fund for the NAACP. She founded the Children's Defense Fund as an organization to advocate for children and families all over the world.

Elders, Joycelyn (1933–) As a pediatric physician, she became the director of public health in Arkansas. She was subsequently appointed U.S. Surgeon General in spite of her outspoken views, particularly her support of sex education for young people.

Ellington, Duke (1899–1974) Jazz musician, band leader, and composer with an innovative musical genius, he wrote nearly a thousand compositions and was elected to the National Institute of Arts and Letters.

Ellison, Ralph (1914–1994) College lecturer, a writer-in-residence at Rutgers University, and a visiting fellow at Yale University, he gained his literary reputation primarily with the publication of *The Invisible Man*, one of the most significant novels of the postwar years.

Evers, Medgar (1926–1963) As a field secretary for the NAACP, he led the fight against segregation at the University of Mississippi and public facilities in Jackson. He was assassinated in front of his home in 1963 and buried in Arlington National Cemetery.

Evers-Williams, Myrlie (1933–) As the widow of Medgar Evers, she initiated and led the fight that resulted in the conviction of a white supremacist for his murder. She famously commented, "Perhaps Medgar did more in death than in life."

Farrakhan, Louis (1933–) As a leader of the Nation of Islam, he gained notoriety for his outspoken, controversial, and critical remarks about blacks and whites in America, which resulted in a public split with Malcolm X.

Fauntroy, Walter (1933–) Pastor, activist, and politician, he led the New Bethel Baptist Church in Washington, D.C. He believed in integrating church and political activism, and became the first delegate to represent D.C. in the U.S. House of Representatives.

Fauset, Jessie Redmon (1882–1961) Emerging as a significant female writer and novelist during the Harlem Renaissance, she was a Phi Beta Kappa graduate of Cornell University and promoted other writers as the literary editor of the NAACP journal, *The Crisis.*

Fitzgerald, Ella (1917–1996) Placed in an orphanage after a traumatic childhood, she ran away and began dancing in nightclubs in Harlem. The "First Lady of Song" won an Apollo amateur night contest and for four decades was the preeminent interpreter of popular song, winning eight Grammys and was awarded the National Medal of Art and the Presidential Medal of Freedom.

Flack, Roberta (1937–) Entering Howard University at fifteen to study classical piano, she was later well known for her smooth R-and-B sound and romantic light jazz. She has won multiple music awards.

Foreman, George (1949–) Initially living a life of petty crime, he began boxing and went on to win an Olympic gold medal. He took the world heavyweight title from Joe Frazier, but lost to Muhammad Ali. He ultimately became a spokesman for a popular barbeque grill.

Forten, Charlotte L. (1837–1914) She was forced to abandon her education at the Salem Normal School in Massachusetts to begin teaching newly freed slaves in South Carolina. She was a critical thinker and is well remembered for her journal and activist-themed articles.

Franklin, Aretha (1942–   ) The "Queen of Soul" is a self-taught piano prodigy who grew up hearing gospel music in her father's church. She left school at sixteen to sing. Winner of many Grammys, she has been a noted professional singer for more than thirty years. She was the first woman inducted into the Rock and Roll Hall of Fame, and she performed at President Obama's inauguration.

Franklin, John Hope (1915–2009) For more than fifty years, he wrote volumes of history and essays. He wrote a definitive history of the African Americans in America as well as critical essays. He served as president of several academic societies, including the American Historical Association.

Garvey, Marcus (1887–1940) He traveled extensively in London and the Caribbean before he founded the Universal Negro Improvement Association in 1914 to promote the self-empowerment of African Americans. With pomp and oratory, he engaged thousands of people to become followers. He later established the Black Star shipping line for trade and emigration to Africa.

Gates, Henry Louis (1950–   ) A correspondent for *TIME* magazine before earning a Ph.D. at Cambridge University, he held teaching chairs at Cornell and Duke universities. One of his books on critical studies earned the American Book Award. He was chairman of the Afro-American Studies at Harvard University and was involved in the production of television shows on African-American life and legacies. He is currently the director of the W. E. B. DuBois Institute for African and African-American Research at Harvard.

Gibson, Althea (1927–2003) She began her sports career by playing paddle tennis on the streets of Harlem and went on to win the World's Women's Singles Tennis Championship at Wimbledon, England.

Giddings, Paula (1947–   ) Journalist, editor, and author, she was the United Negro Fund Distinguished Scholar at Spelman College and Laurie Chair at Rutgers University. She wrote the definitive social and political history of

African-American women and a biography of anti-lynching activist Ida B. Wells. She is a professor of African-American studies at Smith College.

Giovanni, Nikki (1944–   ) Gaining national prominence in the 1960s as a militant poet, she continues to use her sharp-edged writing to describe black feeling, black talk, and black judgment.

Gist, Carole (1970–   ) In 1990 she became the first black woman to capture the title of Miss USA.

Gladwell, Malcolm (1963–   ) A journalist and staff writer for *The New Yorker*, he is the author of numerous international bestsellers. His writings deal with the unexpected implications of research in social sciences and make frequent and extended use of psychology and social psychology. His writing style is accessible, appealing to a general audience.

Golden, Thelma (1965–   ) She knew early that she wanted to work with art. In high school she trained as a curatorial apprentice at the Metropolitan Museum of Art and eventually she became the curator of the Whitney Museum. Currently she serves as the director and chief curator of the Studio Museum of Harlem.

Gordy, Berry, Jr. (1929–   ) Recording industry executive and entrepreneur, he established Motown Records in 1959. The Detroit-based record label grew into a full-fledged entertainment corporation, with many of his talented stars entering the Rock and Roll Hall of Fame.

Graves, Earl (1935–   ) Publisher and corporate executive, he is a highly respected and nationally known authority on black business development. He is the founder and publisher of *Black Enterprise* magazine.

Gregory, Dick (1932–   ) The first nationally recognized African-American comedian, he participated in the civil rights movement, marching in Selma, Alabama, and Washington. He is a popular college lecturer, using humor and a sharp tongue to call attention to the plight of blacks, world health, and hunger.

Guinier, Lani (1950–   ) The first female tenured professor at Harvard Law School. She was nominated by President Clinton for Assistant Attorney General for Civil Rights but was rejected because of her views on the subject.

Gumbel, Bryant (1948–   ) Beginning as a sportscaster for NBC Sports, he became a TV journalist and for fifteen years he was the cohost on NBC's *The Today Show*.

Haley, Alex (1921–1992) After retiring from the Coast Guard, he launched his career as a writer working for *Reader's Digest* and *Playboy*. He collaborated with Malcolm X on his autobiography and later wrote *Roots,* based on a twelve-year search to uncover his family history, which was made into a nationally televised miniseries in 1977.

Hamer, Fannie Lou (1917–1977) The youngest of twenty children in a family of sharecroppers, she was left unemployed after deciding to vote. As a result, she became a leader in the grassroots sector of the civil rights struggle, organizing the Mississippi Freedom Democratic Party and economic cooperatives.

Hansberry, Lorraine (1930–1965) At the age of twenty-eight, she received acclaim for her first play, *A Raisin in the Sun*. She was the first African American to win the New York Drama Critics Circle Award. The play was later adapted for film and revived on Broadway. At her death she left behind other plays, essays, letters, and diaries, many of which which were later published.

Harper, Frances W. (1825–1911) She supported herself from the age of thirteen and became a prominent orator for the Anti-Slavery Society. A founding member of the National Association of Colored Women and a strong proponent of women's suffrage, she wrote ten volumes of poetry and the first short story credited to a black author.

Henson, Matthew (1866–1955) A skilled navigator with a fluent command of the Eskimo language, he accompanied Robert Perry on all of his polar expeditions. Although he was the first to reach the North Pole in 1909, for thirty years he was largely unrecognized until Congress awarded him a duplicate of the silver medal given to Perry.

Height, Dorothy (1912–2010) Accepted but denied entrance to Barnard College in 1929, she used that experience to form her career in social and community activism. She earned a master's degree from New York University and for forty years was the head of the National Council of Negro Women and served as the national president of the Delta Sigma Theta Sorority. For her efforts she was awarded the Medal of Freedom and Congressional Gold Medal.

Hill, Anita (1956–) With a law degree from Yale University, she held several positions in law and government before testifying during the Supreme Court confirmation hearing of Clarence Thomas that he had sexually harassed her while they both worked at the Equal Employment Opportunity Commission. For her testimony she was both vilified and praised by the public and press. She is currently a professor of social policy, law, and women's studies at Brandeis University.

Hines, Gregory (1946–2003) Gregory and his brother Maurice studied dancing at an early age and later formed an act with their father. As a show business veteran and actor, Gregory was best known for his dazzling performances as a tap dancer. He appeared in films, on stage, and television, and earned a Tony Award and Drama Desk Award for *Jelly's Last Jam*.

Hooks, Benjamin (1925–2010) After receiving a law degree and becoming a minister, he pursued a career in law and business, and was active in the civil rights movement during the 1960s. He was the first black appointee to the Federal Communication Commission and for fifteen years presided over the NAACP.

Horne, Lena (1917–2010) She began dancing at the Cotton Club when she was sixteen and toured as a singer and dancer with Noble Sissle. She went to Hollywood, where she was the first black studio contract performer and starred on stage, in films, and television. She was an incomparable entertainer and outspoken social activist.

Hughes, Langston (1902–1967) Although he attended several colleges, he never obtained his degree, but he was a prolific writer with a long, productive literary career. His huge output of work covered a wide range of prose, poetry, drama, music, and journalism.

Hunter-Gault, Charlayne (1942–) One of the first African-American students to attend the University of Georgia (in 1961), she worked as a TV anchor and at the *New York Times* before her big break on the *MacNeil/Lehrer Report* as the national correspondent. As a journalist, she won multiple awards, including two Emmys and a Peabody for excellence in broadcast journalism. She later left her job at CNN to work in South Africa.

Ice-T (Tracy Morrow) (1958–   ) Having a great success as a rapper and recording artist, he often used controversial raps to express social commentary, leading an assault on racism and mainstream sensibilities. He found himself in the center of the debate over rap, violence, and freedom of speech. He has expanded his career into acting and producing in film and television.

Jackson, Janet (1966–   ) Although her brothers were known as singers, she started her career as a television actress. By 1990 she had established herself as a singer and was on the way to superstar status. She has recorded several platinum albums and won numerous music awards.

Jackson, Jesse (1941–   ) A Baptist preacher with a unique cadence to his speech, he is firmly established as a dynamic force for social and political action. As the founder of PUSH (People United to Save Humanity), he was active in the Southern Christian Leadership Conference (SCLC) and a close associate of Martin Luther King Jr., accompanying him on many of the marches.

Jackson, Michael (1958–2010) The "King of Pop," one of the great entertainers of the era, Jackson began singing with his brothers as the lead singer of the Jackson Five. The group signed with Motown and made a string of Top Ten hits. As a solo artist, he branched out to movies and television, but with producer Quincy Jones, his recordings went off the charts.

Jamison, Judith (1956–   ) She began dancing at age six and was later discovered by Agnes de Mille. In 1964 she began her collaboration with Alvin Ailey, as a dancer, administrator, and chorographer. After Ailey's death, she assumed the directorship of the Alvin Ailey American Dance Theater, which continues to excel nationally and internationally in the field of modern dance.

Jemison, Mae C. (1956–   ) As a child, she was fascinated with outer space. She obtained a doctor of medicine degree at Cornell Medical College and later joined the Peace Corps. She was later accepted for NASA and became the first African-American female astronaut.

Johnson, Beverly (1952–   ) In her youth, she was a champion swimmer, with aspirations of becoming a lawyer. At the suggestion of a friend she started to model and obtained work with *Glamour* magazine. She was the first black model to appear on the cover of American *Vogue*. She has done acting in film and television. As a businesswoman, she developed a popular line of wigs and hair care products.

Johnson, Earvin "Magic" (1960–   ) One of the best basketball players ever, he was an all-American at Michigan State University and played for the Los Angeles Lakers from 1979 to 1992. The team took five NBA titles, and he was a three-time MVP. He heads a foundation dedicated to AIDS research and awareness.

Johnson, James Weldon (1881–1938) Novelist, essayist, critic, and poet, he served as U.S. consul to Venezuela, while maintaining a long career with the NAACP. He wrote a novel but, most notably, one of his poems, "Lift Ev'ry Voice and Sing," has often been called the Negro National Anthem.

Johnson, John H. (1918–2005) He turned a five-hundred-dollar loan using his mother's furniture as collateral into a multimillion-dollar business empire, becoming one of the richest man in the United States. For decades he entertained and educated the public, particularly African Americans, about social and political events through his *Ebony* and *Jet* magazines.

Johnson, Virginia (1950–   ) At the age of nineteen, she was among the first members of the Dance Theatre of Harlem and became a prima ballerina with the company. She remained with them for two decades and danced in the major roles of many classical ballets.

Jones, James Earl (1931–   ) An actor known for his resonant voice. As a child he developed a stutter so serious that he could barely speak for years. He overcame the impairment to become an actor on stage, film, and television. He earned Tony awards for his starring turns in the *Great White Hope* and *Fences*. His work spans a wide variety of roles, and he continues to this day to work on Broadway.

Jones, Quincy (1933–   ) With a music career that spans six decades, he was a jazz prodigy who distinguished himself as a trumpeter, music conductor and arranger, TV and record producer, and recipient of twenty-seven

Grammy Awards. He is best known as producer of Michael Jackson's album *Thriller*, which sold 110 million copies worldwide.

Jordan, Barbara (1936–1996) Receiving a J.D. from Boston University, she practiced law in Texas, where she established strong political credentials. After being elected to the U.S. House of Representatives, she was highly visible during the Watergate hearings. After leaving Congress, she taught at Texas University and was a keynote speaker at the Democratic Convention in 1976 and 1992.

Joyner-Kersee, Jackie (1962–) Voted by *Sports Illustrated for Women* magazine as the greatest female athlete of the twentieth century, just ahead of her inspiration, Babe Didrikson Zaharias. She was the first American to win a gold medal in the long jump and the first woman to earn more than 7.000 points in the heptathalon. She won three gold, one silver, and two bronze Olympic medals.

Karenga, Ron (1941–) Author, active with the Black Power movement and former chairman of the Africana Studies Department of California State University, he created a nationally accepted holiday using symbols and practices called "Kwanzaa" to celebrate the African-American family, community, and race between Christmas and the New Year.

King, Coretta Scott (1927–2006) She completed her music degree in voice and violin from New England Conservatory of Music at Boston University and married Martin Luther King Jr. She walked side by side with him during the civil right struggle but emerged as a forceful civil rights leader after his death. Coretta Scott King led the fight to proclaim his birthday as a national day of celebration and founded the Martin Luther King Jr. Center for Nonviolent Social Change in Atlanta, Georgia.

King, Martin Luther, Jr. (1929–1968) The grandson of a slave and the son and grandson of Baptist ministers, he became an ordained pastor. He won worldwide acclaim for his use of nonviolence as an instrument for social change. He was the youngest winner in history of the Nobel Peace Prize and galvanized a nation to conduct the Montgomery bus boycott, resulting in the desegregation in America. He was assassinated in Memphis on April 4, 1968.

Kitt, Eartha (1929–2008) She began her career as a member of the Katherine Dunham Dance Company. Because she was fluent in French and spoke other languages, she developed an international audience. As an actress, singer, and cabaret star, she used her highly distinctive purr-of-a-voice singing style with a slinky stage presence to work on Broadway and in film and television.

Lee, Spike (1957–   ) He attended Morehouse College and film school at New York University, where his early work was first produced. He has created box office successes and gained national recognition covering controversial subjects in films and television.

Lewis, Reginald (1942–1993) A graduate of Harvard Law School, he purchased Beatrice International Foods, a snack food, beverage, and grocery store conglomerate. He became one of the wealthiest black businessmen in the 1980s, making TLC Beatrice International the first black business to earn more than a billion dollars in annual sales. He gave millions of dollars to charitable and political causes.

Lincoln, Abbey (1930–2010) A jazz vocalist, song writer, and actress in films, she wrote and performed her own compositions. In 2003, she received the National Endowment of the Arts Jazz Masters Award.

Love, Ruth B. (1939–   ) Granddaughter of a runaway slave, she received a Ph.D. from United States International University, San Diego, California. She is the former superintendent of the Chicago and San Diego public schools. She is an outspoken advocate of public education reform and improvement in urban schools.

Lorde, Audre (1934–1992) Trained as a librarian, she eventually held the Thomas Hunter Chair in English at Hunter College. She was a poet, feminist, educator, and lesbian activist.

Mabley, Jackie "Moms" (1894–1975) She left home at an early age after being pressured to marry an older man and was a pioneer as a stand-up comedian with triple X-rated material. She was noted for wearing androgynous clothing and was successful on the "chitlin' circuit," earning $10,000 per week at the Harlem Apollo Theatre.

Malcolm X (1925–1965) While serving six years in prison, he converted to Islam and began reading and educating himself about black history. After release, he used his oratory skills and fiery speech to become one of the Nation of Islam's most effective ministers. After his break with the Nation of Islam, he founded the Organization of Afro-American Unity, to provide a less exclusionary forum. He was assassinated on February 21, 1965.

Marshall, Paule (1929–) After graduating Phi Beta Kappa from Brooklyn College, she worked at a small magazine before her first novel was published. She is the author of three additional novels as well as many well-known short stories and has received numerous honors, including awards from the National Endowment of the Arts.

Marshall, Thurgood (1908–1993) The grandson of slaves was denied admission to the University of Maryland Law School but received his law degree from Howard University. As an NAACP lawyer, he won twenty-two cases before the Supreme Court, including *Brown v. Board of Education*. He was the first African American to serve on the Supreme Court, for a period of twenty-four years.

Mays, Benjamin E. (1895–1984) A Baptist minister with a Ph.D. from the University of Chicago, he was elected president of Morehouse College. Throughout his career as an educator, he was committed to civil rights and the education of African-American males, ensuring they graduated not only with an excellent education but also making a commitment to contribute to the race and society.

McMillan, Terry (1951–) As a teenager she developed a love of books by working in her local library. Educated as a journalist and screenwriter, she became the bestselling author of seven novels, three of which have been made into successful television features and films. She is credited with identifying the market for African-American contemporary fiction.

McNair, Ronald (1950–1986) With a Ph.D. in physics from the Massachusetts Institute of Technology and nationally recognized in laser physics, he was one of the thirty-five finalists from an applicant pool of ten thousand for the NASA astronaut program. He was the second African American to fly in space and one of the seven astronauts who died in the launch of the space shuttle *Challenger*.

Miller, Kelly (1863–1939) After serving in the Confederate Army, he became the first black mathematician graduate student admitted to John Hopkins University. He was prevented from continuing after two years because of an increase in tuition. He was professor and dean of the College of Arts and Sciences at Howard University and was an author of numerous articles on race and education.

Morrison, Toni (1931–) She was an editor at Random House when her first novel was published. Her subsequent novels are known for their epic themes, vivid dialogue, and richly detailed black characters. She was awarded the Pulitzer Prize and became the first African-American woman to be awarded the Nobel Prize for Literature. She also has been a professor at major universities.

Muhammad, Elijah (1897–1975) The spiritual leader of the Nation of Islam from 1934 to 1975. For four decades the organization exerted religious and moral influence in the African-American communities, where it established more than 150 temples, restaurants, banks, markets, and industries promoting economic independence.

Murphy, Eddie (1961–) Actor-comedian who starred on late-night television, toured, and performed before sold-out audiences, recorded several best-selling comedy albums, and has played leading roles in blockbuster films.

Nelson, Jill (1952–) For more than twenty years she has been a journalist and novelist, writing for major magazines and newspapers. Her autobiography won the American Book Award, and her novels convey the experiences of middle-class African-American women.

Northrup, Solomon (1809–unknown) A self-educated free man, he was kidnapped and forced into slavery for twelve years but was successful in petitioning for his freedom in 1853. He wrote an extensive account of his experiences, which was published.

Obama, Barack (1961–) A graduate of Harvard Law School, community activist, civil rights attorney, and teacher of constitutional law, he served three terms in the Illinois Senate and was elected to the U.S. Senate before becoming the first African-American president of the United States.

Obama, Michelle (1964–) Wife of the forty-fourth President of the United States and graduate of Harvard Law School, she has become a fashion icon and role model for her notable advocacy for poverty awareness and healthy eating.

Odetta (1930–2008) A singer, actress, guitarist, songwriter, and human rights activist, she was often referred to as the "Voice of the Civil Rights Movement." She was credited with bringing folk songs out of the archives and backwoods into mainstream popular American culture. Work songs, freedom and prison songs, spirituals, and blues were all part of her repertoire.

Owens, Jesse (1913–1980) Born in rural Alabama, Owens earned national recognition in high school and college for his athletic prowess. He earned four gold medals in the 1936 Summer Olympics in Berlin, Germany, in a dramatic rebuttal of Adolf Hitler's perception of white supremacy.

Parker, Charlie (1920–1955) Self-taught saxophonist who learned music listening outside clubs while he was underage. Joining his first band at sixteen, he became a well-regarded jazz artist and revolutionized modern jazz with his amazingly fast, perky, and very bluesy style of playing. In spite of his destructive lifestyle, he was a role model and influenced many younger artists.

Parks, Rosa (1913–2005) This NAACP organizer was credited with helping to start the year-long Montgomery bus boycott by refusing to give up her seat to a white man on a bus in Alabama. In her own quiet way, she worked tirelessly for social reform.

Pennington, James W. (1807–1870) Born a slave, working as a stonemason and blacksmith, he became a fugitive and was looked after by a Quaker who taught him to read and write. He earned a doctor of divinity degree from the University of Heidelberg, Germany, and became an avid abolitionist, lecturing both in the United States and abroad.

Piper, Adrian (1948–) A conceptual artist and analytic philosopher, she completed undergraduate studies in painting and sculpture and later received a Ph.D. from Harvard University in philosophy. Her principal philosophical publications are in metaethics, Kant, and the history of ethics.

Plato, Ann (1820–unknown) Born free of mixed race, she became a school teacher at Black Zion Methodist Church in Hartford, Connecticut. She was the second black woman to publish a book in America and the first to publish a book of essays and poems. Nothing is known about her life after the book was published in 1841.

Powell, Adam Clayton, Jr. (1908–1972) Succeeding his father as the pastor of the Abyssinian Baptist Church, he was the first African American elected to U.S. House of Representatives, where he became chairman of the Education and Labor Committee. He supported the passage of significant social legislation for the benefit of the underclass.

Powell, Colin (1937–) An American statesman and retired four-star general, he was born in Harlem, New York, and received a B.S. in geology. He was the first African American to serve as U.S. Secretary of State. Prior to that he accomplished another first, serving as chairman of the Joint Chiefs of Staff. After retirement, he has devoted his time to philanthropic causes.

Price, Leontyne (1927–) She began playing the piano before discovering her vocal talents as an opera soprano. Her voice was described as brilliant upper register with flowing phrasing and wide dynamic range. She was the first African American to become a leading singer at the Metropolitan Opera and earned fees comparable with the leading opera singers of her day.

Proctor, Samuel D. (1922–1997) A distinguished minister, educator, and author, he became the president of two colleges and professor emeritus of Rutgers University. He was the pastor of Abyssinian Baptist Church for seventeen years, succeeding Adam Clayton Powell Jr., and was noted for mentoring other young ministers.

Queen Latifah (Dana Elaine Owens) (1970–) She began her musical career as a rapper and released her first album at nineteen. She shifted to singing lyrics primarily in soul music and jazz standards. She has gained mainstream success in film and become a celebrity spokesperson for cosmetics, clothing, weight loss, and pizza.

Randolph, A. Philip (1889–1989) As a high school student, he excelled in literature, drama, and public speaking. He founded the *Messenger,* a monthly radical socialist magazine. He later established the Brotherhood of Sleeping

Car Porters and organized the March on Washington, representing a unifying of blacks and whites, preceding the Million Man March.

Reagon, Bernice Johnson (1942–   ) In her youth she was a civil rights advocate and member of the Freedom Singers. She is founder and artistic director of Sweet Honey in the Rock, an a cappella ensemble that performs traditional music of the African Diaspora. She holds the title of curator emeritus at the Smithsonian Institute's National Museum of American History.

Redding, J. Saunders (1906–1988) Literary critic, historian, and education, he was a professor at various colleges and universities before becoming the first African American to hold a faculty position at an Ivy League university. He wrote many books and articles on African-American culture and other topics.

Reed, Ishmael (1938–   ) He briefly attended the University of Buffalo, where he was later awarded an honorary doctorate. As a poet, essayist, and novelist, he attained prominence creating satirical works challenging American-centered culture and highlighting political and cultural oppression. He has written, among others, nine novels, six collections of poetry, eight collections of essays, two travelogues, and six plays. He is noted for his sharp tongue and outrageous titles for his works.

Rice, Condoleezza (1954–   ) Although studying French, music, and ballet with the goal of being a concert pianist, she changed directions to international politics and obtained a Ph.D. in political science from the Korbel School of International Studies at the University of Denver. She became the second African American to serve as U.S. Secretary of State, after Colin Powell, and the second woman to hold that position.

Roach, Max (1924–2007) Roach was one of our greatest drummers. He grew up in a musical family in Brooklyn and at the age of ten was playing drums in gospel bands. He studied classical percussion and was one of the first to play in the bebop style. He developed a flowing rhythmic style and played in many famous jazz groups.

Robeson, Paul (1898–1976) He graduated from Columbia Law School but began his career in the theater as a bass-baritone concert singer and attained fame as a singer and actor. He was the first black actor of the twentieth century to portray Shakespeare's Othello on Broadway. As a political artist, he openly spoke out against fascism and racism, which resulted in persecution and prosecution.

Robinson, Jackie (1919–1972) At UCLA, he played football, basketball, and baseball before serving as an army officer. He played baseball in the Negro League and later signed as the first black player in the Major Leagues with the Brooklyn Dodgers, going on to play in the World Series. With a career average of .311, he was the first black player elected to the Hall of Fame.

Robinson, Rachel (1922–   ) As a professional in psychiatric nursing, she held clinical, teaching, and administrative positions. She is the widow of Jackie Robinson and the founder and chairperson of the Jackie Robinson Foundation for the advancement of higher education among underserved populations.

Rudolph, Wilma (1940–1994) Although disabled as a child with infantile paralysis and later surviving scarlet fever, whooping cough, chicken pox, and measles, she was healthy by the age of twelve and in high school was a basketball star. Competing in the 1960 Olympics, she became the first American woman to win three gold medals in track and field. She was considered the fastest woman in the world at the time.

Russwurm, John Brown (1799–1851) Born to an English gentleman and a black slave, he was acknowledged by his father and was the first African to graduate from Bowdoin College and the third from an American college. He openly opposed slavery and was the cofounder of *Freedom's Journal*, the first African-American newspaper.

Sanchez, Sonia (1934–   ) A poet often associated with the Black Arts Movement, she has authored more than a dozen books of poetry, plays, and children's books. As a professor, she has taught at eight universities and lectured at 500 college campuses across the United States and internationally. She uses her sharp tongue to call attention to the struggles and lives of Black America.

Schomburg, Arthur Alfonso (1874–1938) Determined to disprove his teachers' claims that blacks had no history, heroes, or accomplishments, he studied Negro literature. He began researching and collecting materials, cofounding the Negro Society for Historical Research. The New York Public

Library purchased his extensive collection and appointed him curator of the Schomburg Collection of Negro Literature and Art, which is named in his honor and located in Harlem, New York.

Shange, Ntozake (1948–) Bused to a white school, she endured racism and racist attacks. While she graduated from college *cum laude* and earned a master's degree from the University of Southern California, she suffered from depression and alienation and attempted suicide. She is a poet and essayist whose primary work, *For Colored Girls Who Have Considered Suicide When the Rainbow Is Enuf,* has been presented many times as a stage play, winning multiple awards, and was made into a film by Tyler Perry.

Simmons, Kimora Lee (1975–) After taunts and bullying because of her mixed ancestry and height, she enrolled in modeling classes and as a teenager was awarded a modeling contract. She became the creative director of Baby Phat for women and later became the CEO of Phat Fashions, a highly successful line of urban, hip-hop clothing.

Simone, Nina (1933–2003) A singer, songwriter, pianist, arranger, and civil rights activist. Simone originally aspired to be a classical pianist but her works covered a variety of musical styles, including jazz, blues, soul, folk, R&B, gospel, and pop. Her fifty live and studio albums had a lasting impact on our musical culture.

Sims, Naomi (1948–2009) Although teased about her height and prevented from getting modeling work because of her dark skin, she became the first successful black model appearing on the cover of major magazines, a consummate moment of the Black Is Beautiful movement. She created a successful wig collection and wrote five books on modeling and beauty.

Sinbad (David Adkins) (1956–) Known for his clean comedy, he is a stand-up comic and actor who began performing in the early 1980s, featured in his own HBO special and starred in several films and television shows.

Snoop Dogg (Cordozar Calvin Broadus) (1971–) Entertainer, rapper, recording producer, and actor, he began playing piano and singing in the Baptist church. He is noted for his smooth delivery and violent misogynistic lyrics. After starring in motion pictures and hosting TV shows, he left behind the gangster image.

Sister Souljah (Lisa Williamson) (1964–   ) A prominent rapper and community organizer who grew up in housing projects, she was a political activist at Rutgers University. In her position of influence as a hip-hop artist, she draws attention and criticism because of the inflammatory nature of her comments on race relations.

Sutton, Sharon Egretta (1941–   ) Initially educated in music, she changed her interest and became a registered architect, becoming the second African-American woman elected a fellow in the American Institute of Architects. Her focus is community-based participatory research and design with a special emphasis on low-income, minority youth and other disenfranchised populations.

Taylor, Susan (1946–   ) Although she had not attended college as a licensed cosmetologist, she understood the specific needs and concerns of black women. She was hired at *Essence* magazine as the beauty editor and moved up the ranks to become the editor-in-chief. She is a public speaker and has written many articles and books on the empowerment of women.

Terrell, Mary Church (1863–1954) Daughter of slaves, she was one of the first African-American women to earn a college degree and be appointed to a board of education. She became a tireless activist for civil rights and suffrage as a founding member of the Niagara Movement and NAACP and the first president of the National Association of Colored Women.

Thomas, Clarence (1948–   ) A graduate of Yale Law School, he held a number of political posts before being nominated to the U.S. Circuit Court of Appeals. A year later he was nominated to the Supreme Court to fill the position left by Thurgood Marshall. After volatile hearings, he was confirmed by the U.S. Senate.

Thurman, Howard (1899–1981) A graduate of Morehouse College and Dean of Theology at Howard University and Boston University, he was a prolific author, writing twenty books on ethical and cultural criticism. His works and spiritual advising inspired many of our community leaders.

Toomer, Jean (1894–1967) A graduate of University of Wisconsin and City College of New York, he traveled widely before taking a position as a principal in Sparta, Georgia, the setting for his single novel, *Cane.* It was one of the landmarks of the Harlem Renaissance and considered a classical work.

Truth, Sojourner (1797–1883) She could neither read nor write, but after receiving freedom from the New York State Emancipation Act, she won a national reputation for her powerful lectures against slavery and as an advocate for those who remained slaves in other states. After national emancipation, she was a strong proponent of equal rights for both African Americans and women.

Tubman, Harriet (1820–1913) After escaping from slavery at the age of twenty-five, she returned South nineteen times to spirit three hundred people to Canada on the Underground Railroad. She supported women's rights and during the Civil War served as a nurse, spy, and scout for the Union Army.

Turner, Tina (1939–   ) Born in rural Tennessee, she sang in church choirs and local contests. After marriage, she enjoyed a string of hit records, but dropped out after years of abuse and divorce. She returned to recording and achieved acclaim, winning several Grammy awards. With a career spanning fifty years, she is considered the Queen of Rock and Roll.

Vereen, Ben (1946–   ) A versatile entertainer whose talents include singer-dancer, comedian, and serious actor. He has appeared in numerous Broadway theater shows and performed in one-man shows. He was nominated for a Tony Award for *Jesus Christ Superstar,* and won a Tony Award for *Pippin.*

Walker, Alice (1944–   ) A graduate of Sarah Lawrence College, she became interested in the civil rights movement and wrote poetry and her first novel as a student. Her subsequent novels and works of poetry speak to issues of race and gender. Her most famous and critically acclaimed novel, *The Color Purple,* won the Pulitzer Prize for Fiction.

Walker, David (1783–1830) An author of one of the most powerful documents in early American history. As a fervent abolitionist, his Appeal was a condemnation of slavery recalling the founding principles of the republic and posed the threat of armed insurrection.

Walker, Madam C. J. (1867–1919) She was orphaned at seven, married at fourteen, and widowed at twenty. She became a businesswoman, hair care entrepreneur, and philanthropist. She developed her own hair products, which were marketed throughout the United States, and launched a cosmetology school, which made her the first self-made woman millionaire in America.

Walker, Margaret (1915–1998) With a master's degree in creative writing and a Ph.D. from University of Iowa, she was a poet and writer. She founded the Institute of History, Life, and Culture of Black People and wrote books of poetry and novels, of which her most popular was *Jubilee,* based on her own great-grandmother's life as a slave. She released three albums of poetry.

Washington, Denzel (1954–　) Actor, screenwriter, director, and producer who has garnered much acclaim for his film work portraying real-life figures. He has been awarded two Golden Globes, a Tony, and two Academy Awards. He is the second African-American male to win an Academy Award for best actor.

Washington, Booker T. (1856–1915) He was born into slavery but after emancipation worked his way through Hampton Normal and Agriculture Institute, where he returned as a teacher. He was the organizer of the National Business League and founder of Tuskegee Institute. He felt obtaining wealthy white support was the best way to confront racism, which he used to educate and empower blacks but proved controversial.

Wattleton, Faye (1943–　) She trained as a nurse and earned a master of science degree in maternal and infant care, with certification as a nurse-midwife from Columbia. She became the first African-American and youngest president elected to Planned Parenthood, where she served fourteen years.

Wells-Barnett, Ida B. (1862–1931) Born into slavery and a college dropout, she found employment as a teacher in a black school. She was a journalist, newspaper editor, and early leader in the civil rights movement. She documented and spoke out boldly about the extent of lynching in the United States. She was also active in the women's rights and suffrage movement.

West, Cornel (1953–　) An ordained minister, professor of religion, and director of Afro-American Studies at Princeton University, and professor of African American Studies and the Philosophy of Religion at Harvard, he is a charismatic speaker and analytic writer on issues of morality, race relations, cultural diversity, and progressive politics.

Wheatley, Phillis (1753–1784) Enslaved at the age of eight, she was tutored by her owner's daughter and learned to read and write English in sixteen months. She continued her studies with Greek and Latin classics as well as readings from the the Bible. She became the first African-American woman in U.S. history to have her poetry published.

White, Walter (1883–1955) A civil rights activist, he participated in the local branch of the NAACP after graduation from Atlanta University. He joined the NAACP in 1918 and served for twenty-four years as national executive secretary. He spent a lifetime investigating riots and lynchings around America, in addition to being a writer of a syndicated newspaper column, fiction, and nonfiction.

Wilkins, Roger (1932–   ) A civil rights leader, professor of history, and journalist, Wilkins received a law degree at the University of Michigan. He became an Assistant Attorney General to President Lyndon Johnson, serving as one of the highest-ranking blacks in the executive branch at that time. He later worked on the editorial staff of the *Washington Post,* where he shared a Pulitzer Prize for reporting on the Watergate scandal. He is the nephew of the past executive director of NAAC, Roy Wilkins, and is currently a history professor at George Mason University.

Wilkins, Roy (1901–1981) A civil rights activist, he succeeded Walter White as the executive of the NAACP and then became the editor of *The Crisis* magazine. He led the organizing of alliances with other rights groups in a rapidly changing political environment, including the Brotherhood of Sleeping Car Porters, and founded the Leadership Conference on Civil Rights.

Williams, Vanessa (1963–   ) A singer and actress who studied piano and French horn. She discontinued her education at Syracuse University to become the first African American to be crowned Miss America, a title she relinquished due to a scandal. She rebounded, launching a career with Grammy, Emmy and Tony Awards nominations. Twenty-five years after leaving Syracuse, she obtained her degree.

Wilmore, Gayraud (1921–   ) He interrupted his studies at Lincoln University to become a Buffalo Soldier with the all-black 92nd Infantry division in Italy. After service, he studied for the ministry. He has written sixteen books as a scholar in theology and religious history of African Americans.

Wilson, August (1945–2005) An avid reader, he dropped out of high school and educated himself by extensive use of the Carnegie Library, which later awarded him a degree. He established a literary legacy by writing ten plays,

The Pittsburgh Cycle, for which earned two Pulitzer Prizes and five New York Drama Critics Circle awards for best plays. Each play is set in a different decade, depicting the comic and tragic aspects of African-American experience in the twentieth century.

Winfrey, Oprah (1954–) Through a troubled childhood, she excelled in school and obtained a full scholarship to Tennessee State University, where she studied communications. She began work in radio and television and quickly rose to have her own syndicated show, which has made her one of the world's wealthiest and most popular entertainers. She headed her own production company and starred in television and films.

Wolfe, George C. (1954–) A playwright with a MFA in dramatic writing and musical theater from New York University, he took over the reins of the New York Shakespeare Festival/Public Theater. He has gained national recognition for his writing, directing, and producing of off-Broadway and Broadway work and has won two Tony Awards.

Woodson, Carter G. (1875–1950) The son of a former slave, he was unable to attend school until the age of twenty and ultimately received a Ph.D. from Harvard University. He was the founder of the Association for the Study of African American Life and History. He was an author and journalist who was one of the first scholars of Negro history, organizing Negro History Week and Black History Month.

Wright, Richard (1908–1960) Growing up in extreme poverty and forced to leave school to work, he became a powerful author of sometimes controversial novels, short stories, and nonfiction. His vivid depiction of racial themes helped to define discussions on race relations in the mid-twentieth century.

Young, Andrew (1932–) Although beginning his studies in pre-dentistry, he altered his course to the ministry and was a close associate of Dr. Martin Luther King Jr. in the civil rights movement. He served as the Georgia representative to Congress, was appointed ambassador to the United Nations, and served as mayor of Atlanta.

INDEX

INDEX

INDEX

ACKNOWLEDGMENTS

My thanks to:

Barbara Lowenstein, my agent, who recommended me when Esther Margolis, president of Newmarket Press, asked if Linda Villarosa would be interested in the book project. Barbara replied she didn't think Linda was available, but suggested Linda's mother as a good prospect.

Esther Margolis, who recognized me from my activity as a bookseller and felt I would be an excellent alternative to Linda.

Keith Hollaman, my editor, who was supportive, offering kind words and reassurance after each submission.

Shannon Holden Ayers, my friend in Dubai, who was my reader and provided support and constructive criticism, thanks to the Internet and Skype.

Jane Small, a friend who listened to my fussing and ventilating.

Sharon Howard and the staff of Schomburg Center for Research in Black Culture, who were helpful in guiding me through the library system.

Anita King, who was volunteering at the Schomburg and encouraged me "to go for it," as she had traveled the road before.

My daughters, Alicia and Linda, and my grandchildren, Kali and Nicholas, for being a loving family.

—Clara Villarosa

ABOUT THE EDITOR

Clara Villarosa opened The Hue-Man Experience bookstore in Denver, specializing in African-American titles, more than two decades ago and later opened a second, enormously successful branch in Harlem.

The recipient of more than thirty awards, including the National Minority Entrepreneur of the Year, she lives in Harlem, New York. A business coach, she is the author of *Down to Business: The First 10 Steps to Entrepreneurship for Women.*

THE ACCLAIMED NEWMARKET *WORDS OF* SERIES

The Words of Extraordinary Women
Selected and Introduced by Carolyn Warner
A celebration of the most important female voices in history, this uplifting and thought-provoking compendium features quotes from notable women on the arts, education, success, and politics; 176 pages.

The Words of Abraham Lincoln
Selected and Introduced by Larry Shapiro
A collection of wise and inspiring quotations from the speeches and writings of Abraham Lincoln covering the slavery controversy, the Civil War, and his personal life. Includes photographs, chronology; 128 pages.

The Words of Albert Schweitzer
Selected and Introduced by Norman Cousins
An inspiring collection focusing on: Knowledge and Discovery, Reverence for Life, Faith, The Life of the Soul, The Musician as Artist, and Civilization and Peace. Includes photographs, chronology, excerpt from acceptance speech for the 1954 Nobel Peace Prize; 112 pages.

The Words of Desmond Tutu
Selected and Introduced by Naomi Tutu
Nearly 100 memorable quotations from the addresses, sermons, and writings of South Africa's Nobel Prize–winning archbishop. Topics include: Faith and Responsibility, Apartheid, Family, Violence and Nonviolence, The Community—Black and White, and Toward a New South Africa. Includes photographs, chronology, text of acceptance speech for the 1984 Nobel Peace Prize; 112 pages.

The Words of Gandhi
Selected and Introduced by Sir Richard Attenborough
More than 150 selections from the letters, speeches, and writings, collected in five sections—Daily Life, Cooperation, Nonviolence, Faith, and Peace. Includes *TIME* magazine's millennium essay on Gandhi's impact on the twentieth century; photographs, chronology, bibliography, glossary; 128 pages.

The Words of Martin Luther King, Jr.
Selected and Introduced by Coretta Scott King
More than 120 quotations and excerpts from the great civil rights leader's speeches, sermons, and writings on: The Community of Man, Racism, Civil Rights, Justice and Freedom, Faith and Religion, Nonviolence, and Peace. Includes photographs, chronology, text of presidential proclamation of King holiday; 128 pages.

The Words of Peace
Selections from the Speeches of the Winners of the Nobel Peace Prize
Selected and Edited by Professor Irwin Abrams. Foreword by President Jimmy Carter
A new compendium of excerpts from award winners' acceptance speeches spanning 1901 to 2007, including Al Gore, the Dalai Lama, Mother Teresa, Lech Walesa, Martin Luther King Jr., and Elie Wiesel. Themes are: Peace, Human Rights, Violence and Nonviolence, The Bonds of Humanity, and Faith and Hope. Includes photographs, biographical notes, chronology, and index; 176 pages.

Newmarket Press books are available from your local or online bookseller or from Newmarket Press, Special Sales Department, 18 East 48th Street, New York, NY 10017; phone 212-832-3575 or 800-669-3903; fax 212-832-3629; e-mail info@newmarketpress.com. Prices and availability are subject to change. Catalogs and information on quantity order discounts are available on request.

www.newmarketpress.com